JOHN

The Gospel of Faith

By

EVERETT F. HARRISON

MOODY PRESS • CHICAGO

Copyright ©, 1962, by
THE MOODY BIBLE INSTITUTE
OF CHICAGO

ISBN: 0-8024-2043-5

Printed in the United States of America

2 95

JOHN

The Gospel of Faith

PREFACE

A WORD OF EXPLANATION is due the reader concerning the nature of the treatment of the Fourth Gospel contained in these pages.

The objective has been to get at the essential thought in each section rather than to draw out the lessons which may suggest themselves. No attempt has been made in the direction of illustration and almost none in the area of application.

It will be readily seen, therefore, that if the reader is to profit from the approach made here, he should by all means keep the text of the Gospel before him as he proceeds.

—EVERETT F. HARRISON

CONTENTS

INTRODUCTION

OF ALL THE BOOKS of the New Testament, the one which has commanded the greatest interest and devotional attachment is the Gospel according to John. The scholar may study it chiefly because of its problems, and the ordinary believer because of its power to feed his soul, but in either case the Gospel continues to be the center of attention.

It is well to be reminded that this is a Gospel. This is a writing deliberately intended to set forth the saving message of the Christian faith as it centers in the historic figure of Jesus of Nazareth. It is not a life of Christ any more than the other Gospels. In fact, it is even less so, for the movements of Jesus are fewer and the actual events much more limited.

Some of the leading characteristics of the Gospel may be recalled. Everywhere the person of Christ as the Son of God receives recurrent emphasis. From the very beginning His relation to the Father comes into view, and shortly the grand truth of His incarnation is spread before the reader. A few miracles, chosen out of many, dot the pages of the narrative, and these are usually closely connected with a discourse by our Lord which has some bearing on the miracle. This arrangement honors the truth that revelation is both by deed and by word. Both of these make their contribution to the conclusion that Jesus is the Christ, the Son of God.

But the writing is not simply factual; it is openly evangelistic. The writer presses for a verdict. To believe in the Son brings eternal life. The consequence of refusal to believe is just as clearly spelled out. To reject Christ is to perish.

A strongly marked feature is the stubborn opposition to the claims of Jesus by the Jewish authorities. They have ample opportunity to hear Him and to know of the signs which He performs, but for various reasons they fail to respond to Him. Once they are convinced that He is a blasphemer, a mere man pretending to be the Son of God, their eyes and ears are closed to evidence. This is the more pitiable in view of the barrenness of the religious system to which they are committed, and the writer is at some pains to disclose this emptiness at various points in the narrative.

Those who see in this Gospel also a polemic against gnosticism are probably correct. This system of thought could not tolerate the idea of an incarnation and found the truth of our Lord's humanity unacceptable. John counters with stress upon the "flesh" of the Son of man.

The longest discourse in the Gospel relates the teaching of Jesus to the disciples in the Upper Room. Nothing of this sort appears in the other evangelists. Here the life of the church is anticipated and the divine resources for that life are spelled out. A note of poignancy and tenderness is present throughout in view of the impending separation between the Lord and His own.

In the ancient church at least one writer characterized this as the "spiritual" Gospel. This could be defended

10

from the standpoint of preoccupation with spiritual truth and also from the fact that the Holy Spirit is given such a large place. Certainly there is a type of thought which may be designated as Johannine, and it is justifiably called spiritual, even though one might be hard pressed to define it more narrowly and exactly.

One of the most obvious features of the Fourth Gospel is its almost total dissimilarity from the Synoptics (Matthew, Mark, Luke). True, it magnifies the same Person and includes some of the same events, especially the events of the passion and resurrection, but much of the material is unique. The center of the ministry is Judea rather than Galilee. Jesus' teaching is largely in discourses centering in Himself rather than in the messages to the multitudes, flavored with parables, with which the Synoptics abound. The cleansing of the temple is located at the beginning of the ministry, whereas the Synoptics place it at the close. We need not suppose a contradiction here, provided room can be found, as it likely can, for two such cleansings. A thorny problem relates to chronology. Whereas the Synoptics appear to put the death of Jesus on the Passover, John seems to place it on the eve of Passover. A recent study may provide the answer to this riddle. Massey H. Shepherd, Jr., believes that the Jews of the Dispersion were obliged to operate on a fixed calendar for the determination of the time of the Jewish feasts, whereas the Jews in Palestine depended upon observation of the new moon. Further, he concludes that in the year of our Lord's death (A.D. 30), the Palestinian Jews observed the Passover on Saturday, and the writer of the Fourth Gospel, who is plainly at home in the Palestinian tradition of Judaism, follows this chronology, whereas the Synoptists, who write from the standpoint of Dispersion Judaism, reproduces the practice of the Jews outside the land, who observed Passover on Friday that year. Shepherd's article, "Are Both the Synoptics and John Correct About the Date of Jesus' Death?" appears in the "Journal of Biblical Literature," June 1961, pp. 123-132.

Although the Gospel itself does not tell us openly who the writer is, we learn from Chapter 21 that he was one of the apostolic circle and a close friend of Simon Peter. John the son of Zebedee fits these requirements. Furthermore, the testimony of the Church Fathers is explicit on this point. Nothing adduced by modern scholarship makes this identification impossible, though many men favor the idea that a disciple of John was the actual writer, incorporating the thoughts and teaching of his master.

Recent study makes it probable that the Gospel was written in Ephesus some time in the last quarter of the first Christian century, directed primarily toward the Jews of the Dispersion as its prospective readers, but also mindful of the needs of all men and of the sufficiency of Christ, the Son of God, to meet them.

The following outline gives only the broad divisions of the book. A more detailed analysis accompanies the exposition.

OUTLINE

I. Prologue   (1:1-18).

II. The Witness of the Son of God to the World
   (1:19—12:50).

III. The Witness of the Son of God to His Own
   (13:1—17:26).

IV. The Witness of the Son of God in Obedience to
   the Father unto Death   (18:1—19:42).

V. The Witness of the Risen Lord   (20:1-31).

VI. Epilogue   (21:1-25).

I. Prologue (1:1-18)

THIS GOSPEL, like the others, is a message about Jesus Christ. All the Gospels except Luke mention Him in the first verse of their accounts. John's title for the Great Subject is special and unique. *Word* is an attempt to translate Logos, which has a variety of meanings, including reason and revelation. The latter sense is prominent in the prologue. Observe how Word is surrounded by terms which suggest disclosure and communication—light—lighteth—shineth (vss. 9, 5); glory (vs. 14); declared (vs. 18).

John's opening words are the same as those of Genesis—the new creation looks back to the old for a starting point before moving beyond it. In a few compact sentences the Word is seen in relation to God (vss. 1, 2), to the Creation (vs. 3), and to men (vss. 4, 5). As to the first, the fellowship of the Word with God is based on equality with God, participation in the Godhead without confusion of persons. The one who reveals God fully, not fragmentarily, must be no less than God (cf. Heb. 1:1-4). The Word is God's agent (*by him*) in creation (so in Col. 1:16; Heb. 1:2). Nothing has emerged of itself or in response to some other creative power. With respect to *men,* the Word is the one hope for the realization of the goal of their creation (spiritual *life*). The *darkness* and *light* of the creation story take on more than physical significance

14

here. Darkness spells ignorance of God and separation from Him because of sin. *Comprehended* may suggest grasping with the mind and also grasping so as to resist or eliminate. Both are true to Scripture teaching.

The Word had a special preparatory witness in John (the Baptist), who, though a light, is the lesser light sent to point men to the Light par excellence (vss. 6-9). As men receive his *witness* they will be ready to *believe* in the Greater Light that rules the day of full-orbed revelation. As John carried on his work, the *true* (perfect, ultimate) Light was even then coming into the world. The dawning rays were on the point of flooding the forlorn lowlands where darkness reigned.

When the Word was revealed in flesh, the world rejected, but some received Him (vss. 10-14). No fault could be found with His credentials, for He came as Creator and Lord of His inheritance (vss. 10-11). Note the subtle shift in meaning of *world* from the created order to men as God's creatures (vs. 10). John's Gospel spells out as no other does the crisis of confrontation. What will men do with Jesus the Christ? "His own received him not ... as many as received him. ..." This is the dual response traced throughout the book. Those who *believe* (a dominant word in this Gospel) show it by receiving Him. This simple act of faith brings the new status of *sons of God,* born into His family. They are supernaturally born in their way as the Word was born in His (vss. 13-14). What did believers encounter in Christ? Nothing less than a mystery more profound than their own salvation—God had become flesh. The language is deliberately chosen to emphasize that the humanity of Jesus was no phantom. Nor was His residence among men a fleeting thing. He came to dwell. This suggests the permanence of the incarnation. It fits in with an age-old purpose of God to be with His people (Ex. 29:46; II Cor. 6:16; Rev. 21:3). *Dwelt* is literally "tabernacled," and suggests, among other things, the movement of revelation. He moved about among the people as the revelation of God in their midst. As the tabernacle in the wilderness had the glory-cloud to symbolize the divine presence, so this new manifestation has glory, but not something physical. Here shone the light of the divine nature expressing itself as *grace and truth* (cf. vs. 17).

John the Baptist recognized the eminence of Christ before He appeared (vs. 15). *Preferred* denotes superior worth; *before me* suggests the eternal existence of the Son, who was younger in His earthly life than John. The fullness of grace in Christ is communicable —something received, one manifestation of grace heaped upon another (vs. 16). What Christ came to bring was not *law,* but *grace* which has a message for lawbreakers. The law was not contrary to *truth,* but it was not all the truth. God's final revelation was in His Son, who is an only Son (the best Greek manuscripts have *God* rather than *Son*). *Declared* is a colorful word. It means to lead out. From it is derived the word "exegete." The Son explains the Father to those who have not and cannot see God. As the writer of the Epistle to the Hebrews puts it, God spoke through His Son (1:2).

II. The Witness of the Son of God to the World (1:19—12:50)

1. The Introductory Witness of John (1:19-34). Already the prologue has summarized that witness. Now it is given in greater detail. Since John's father was a priest, the deputation from the temple hierarchy expected cooperation in trying to get a self-appraisal from John. He insisted on turning it into an opportunity to exalt the Coming One. Naturally he denied being the Christ. He had no consciousness of being Elijah either (whom the Jews expected to return on the basis of Malachi 4:5, 6), even though Jesus later on gave him that office (Matt. 11:14). Nor was he the *prophet* Moses said would come (Deut. 18:15-18).

The most John would consent to claim for himself was the function of a *voice* sounding out his warning that the covenant nation must get ready for the Lord. This commission he had found in Isaiah 40:3.

Such a modest office did not seem to fit well with John's activity as the baptizer. How could he defend himself on this score? John's answer was that his baptism, in keeping with his place in the divine purpose, was preparatory, a baptism with water, something outward, in the flesh. Right here we expect the contrast with the *Coming One* which is given at the end of

17

verse 33, but that answer is delayed in order to make way for further testimony to Him. John is not worthy to be His servant (vs. 27). These things took place at a spot beyond Jordan. The best attested reading is not Bethabara but Bethany, to be distinguished from the Bethany near Jerusalem (cf. 11:18). The exact location is unknown.

At length Jesus and John meet (vs. 29). The occasion calls for a great pronouncement. Look well, for here is *the Lamb of God* who is to bear in His own Person the world's sin. What is the background of such an assertion? Having found his own calling set forth in Isaiah 40, John had not much further to go to find the mission of Jesus in the work of the Suffering Servant of Isaiah 53. True, the Servant is there compared to "a lamb" in connection with His submission, but the chapter is so full of the taking away of the sins of the many by means of this One that the passage could well be the seed-plot for John's utterance. The paschal lamb of Exodus 12 is less likely as the background here, seeing that this lamb did not take away sin but only served to memorialize what God had done in delivering His people.

John had been in the wilderness for many a year (Luke 1:80), whereas Jesus had grown up in the village of Nazareth. The two had not seen each other, at least not for years. Some identification was needed to help John, and it was provided in the dove-like shape assumed by the Spirit in descending and remaining on Him. Thus was marked out from all others the One who would complete John's work by baptizing with the

Spirit (cf. Acts 1:5). It was one thing to be filled with the Spirit (Luke 1:15) and quite another to be able to direct the operations of the Spirit (John 16:7-15). *Son of God* is the second title attributed to Jesus by John (vs. 34). It echoes the testimony of the Father at the baptism (Mark 1:11).

2. The Witness to Prospective Disciples (1:35-51). It was not in the plan of God, for various reasons, that the Baptist should find a place for himself in the circle of apostles, but he was able to contribute several of his followers to that glorious company. So strong was his testimony to Jesus that men who had walked with John were now drawn to the Saviour. The two who started the trend were Andrew and another who was almost certainly John the son of Zebedee. One question led to another. *What seek ye?* There was no rebuff here, so the two countered, "Rabbi [teacher], *where dwellest thou?*" This was the equivalent of a request for an audience. Long afterward John still recalled the hour (vs. 39). It was a day of indelible impressions. Time notices in the Gospels usually follow the Jewish method of calculation. If the same is done here, the hour was four in the afternoon. In this instance the Roman calculation may be employed —ten in the morning, allowing several hours of conference.

A chain reaction set in. Andrew lost no time finding his brother Simon. The word *first* is ambiguous, but it may well suggest that shortly afterward John found *his* brother James and introduced him to the Master.

19

With Simon before him, Jesus uttered an appraisal (Simon) and a prophecy (stone or piece of rock). Three years were required for the hardening process, but it was achieved by the Day of Pentecost (Acts 2).

Next, Jesus himself took a hand in the business of finding men. He secured the allegiance of a Galilean named Philip (6:5-7; 14:8-10), who in turn won Nathaniel, who had doubts at first that the little hamlet of Nazareth could produce Israel's hope (Andrew had used the term Messiah; Philip simply referred to the prophetic expectation of one whom God would send). Not caring to argue, Philip wisely suggested personal contact with Jesus. The Lord won Nathaniel by showing that He knew what was in this man's inner life and thought. This revelation drew from Nathaniel a confession of Jesus' divine sonship and Messiahship. If he himself was a true Israelite according to Jesus' standard, the Master was Israel's king (vs. 49). Thus did another Galilean put himself under the banner of Christ. To him and the others Jesus gave assurance of further and greater revelation of Himself (vs. 51; cf. 3:12). Discipleship was to bring the thrill of an ever increasing knowledge of the One who was the true ladder between earth and Heaven, the Son of Man. This title breathes deity, not from the term itself, but from the way it is used. The Mediator must be divine, even the man Christ Jesus (I Tim. 2:5). Jacob's vision at Bethel was now to be realized in the person of One upon whom angels waited, but who Himself came to minister to the children of men.

3. The witness at the marriage feast in Cana (2: 1-12). Having just declared Himself to be the Son of Man, Jesus now shows that His tabernacling among men included His sympathetic help. *The third day* is probably reckoned from 1:43, as the intermediate day would be required for the northward journey. Curiously, Jesus' contacts are with His mother and the servants of the household rather than with the principals of the wedding or the other guests. Mary notified Him of the shortage of wine. She may have felt personally responsible, for it is probable that the unexpected arrival of Jesus and His disciples brought through her a last-minute invitation to them. Their presence had helped to deplete the supply of wine.

Jesus' rebuff of His mother (vs. 4) was not personal; He may have sensed an eagerness in her for a dramatic manifestation of His power which would launch Him on His kingly career (cf. Luke 1:32, 33). But His *hour* had not yet come—the hour of His suffering which must precede His triumph (cf. 7:6, 30; 8:20; 12:23; 13:1; 17:1). This gentle rebuke was a reminder to Mary that her son was now a man. She could no longer tell Him what to do. But she could tell *the servants* to comply with any request He might make of them. She felt sure He would intervene in some way (vs. 5).

Attention shifts to *six waterpots of stone.* These were large, containing twenty gallons or more. Apparently they were empty, a picture of Judaism's emptiness despite all its concern for purification. *Fill—draw out.* The first command had to do with water, the second with wine. In between lay the miracle wrought by the creative word of Christ. Ordinarily men found old wine better than the new (Luke 5:39). Not so here. Nothing that comes from the Lord can be less than the best.

The turning of water into wine was *the beginning of miracles* for Jesus. Clearly, then, He performed nothing miraculous in His boyhood. Just as clearly, further miracles were due to come. John's term for miracle is *sign*—the outward and visible points to an even greater inward and spiritual reality. This sign *manifested* His *glory* (cf. 1:14). He showed His grace by intervening with His timely aid. He showed His truth by the sterling quality of that which He produced. Not all profited from the miracle. The guests and the one who presided over the festivities *knew not* what had occurred (cf. 1:10). Mary *hoped* for a miracle; the servants *knew* it had occurred, but the disciples *believed*. Their confidence in Christ took on greater dimensions than before. This is no small part of discipleship.

4. The witness in the cleansing of the temple (2:13-25). This was preceded by a brief sojourn at Capernaum, headquarters for the Galilean ministry (cf. Matt. 4:13).

Passover was one of the three annual festivals which male Jews were expected to attend (the others were Pentecost and Tabernacles). People could not very well bring with them their animals for sacrifice; they must buy them at Jerusalem. At the same time they could conveniently pay their annual dues for the support of the temple. For this purpose they must resort to the moneychangers who would exchange whatever coinage the people brought (they came from all parts of Palestine and many foreign lands) into the one coinage acceptable for the temple tax. The priestly hierarchy arranged for all these transactions to be made in the temple itself, in the court of the Gentiles, and of course they reaped a financial profit for permitting the merchants to take up this advantageous position. Jesus' resentment was kindled by this abuse of the sacred precincts. It meant the turning of His Father's house (cf. Luke 2:49, A.S.V.) into a *house of merchandise.* So He forcibly expelled them. The act recalled to the minds of the disciples an ancient saying (Psalm 69:9) which seemed appropriately fulfilled in Jesus' action. This initial act of His ministry in the holy city proclaimed the nature of His mission. He would strike at all abuses of Judaism.

On the positive side His coming would mean not merely the cleansing of the temple but the supplanting of it by His own person (vs. 21). The Jews would make an attempt to destroy the temple of His body, but they would be unsuccessful, for the resurrection *in three days* would thwart them. By means of the living Christ true worshipers now draw near to God. The age when animal sacrifice was appropriate has come to an end (cf. the argument of the Epistle to the Hebrews). After His resurrection the disciples recalled His words and found new light thrown thereby on Old Testament Scripture, especially such a passage as Psalm 16:10, which predicted no corruption for God's Holy One. It was held that corruption occurred after three days (cf. John 11:39).

The visit to Jerusalem was the occasion for the working of various miracles (vs. 23). Right here we are confronted by a situation which is repeated more than once in this Gospel. Men are said to believe in Christ, but what is said further about them rules them out as genuine believers (cf. 6:66; 8:31-59; 12:42-43). Such people do not reject Christ outright. They are attracted to Him, but only superficially, being impressed by His works or words but not by His worth. Jesus saw their hearts and refused to *commit* (the same word in the original as *believe*) Himself to them (vs. 24). Yet there was hope that some of these miracle-believers could be brought to a place of trust in Christ Himself. We learn of one such in the next chapter. Christ was willing to deal with him.

5. The witness to Nicodemus (3:1-21). This man was a member of the Sanhedrin, the high court of the Jews. His position made any contact with Jesus hazardous, now that relations between the Lord and the authorities had become strained (cf. 2:18). So he came under cover of darkness. John may intend more. *By night* may suggest the spiritual darkness which encompasses the thinking of this leader. He tries to be complimentary, but finds it difficult without being condescending (vs. 2). He is ready to concede that Jesus is a divinely authenticated teacher. He had grasped

24

the truth that words and deeds illuminate one another. Neither should be viewed in isolation.

Jesus' reply takes the conversation immediately beyond pleasantries and plunges it into man's central spiritual problem—how he can be right with God. Says Jesus the teacher, man must be *born again* if he would see *the kingdom of God.* The idea is not at all of a second physical birth such as Nicodemus mentions in his perplexity (vs. 4). *Again* is more accurately rendered *anew.* The word may also mean *from above* (3:31). A birth of a special kind is in view here, requiring an act of God. Birth according to the natural pattern would accomplish little. One might avoid some mistakes in a second chance, but he would still be a sinner. He needs desperately the life of God in order to rise above the limitations of his Adamic nature.

Without the new birth one is unable to see or enter the kingdom of God. This phrase, so common in the Synoptic Gospels, occurs in John only here and in verse 5 (there is an allusion to Jesus' kingdom in 18:36). Entrance to the sphere of God's sovereign rule depends upon spiritual transformation—*born of water and the Spirit.* Water denotes the cleansing from defilement and points to the significance of John's baptism. This is the negative or preparatory side of the new birth. The positive side is accomplished by the Spirit (cf. Luke 1:35 for a parallel).

The necessity for the new birth—ye *must* be born again (vs. 7)—lies in this, that flesh, our human nature in its weakness and sinfulness, can produce only

25

what is like it—more flesh. One cannot get over into the realm of spirit (participation in the life of God, I Cor. 6:17) apart from the new birth.

Nicodemus had voiced his perplexity about such teaching. Now Jesus grants its mysterious character and at the same time affirms its reality as something that has observable effects (vs. 8). Incidentally, *wind* is the same word as Spirit. By this time the visitor is floundering beyond his depth (vs. 9). Jesus informs him that there are other mysteries of a heavenly sort (and He is qualified to expound them because He has seen and known them) in distinction from the new birth, which takes place on earth. No mere man can rise up to glimpse or master these supernal wonders. But one has come down from Heaven with the answers. He speaks, of course, of Himself. The last clause of verse 13 lacks sufficient manuscript authority to be accepted as part of the text.

On what basis does God grant the new birth to men? This is set forth in terms of an Old Testament analogy. The brazen serpent in the wilderness was like the fiery serpents but lacked their destructive power (cf. Rom. 8:3). Moses was commanded to raise it aloft on a pole (Num. 21:8). Thus was anticipated the lifting up of Christ on the Cross as the substitute for sinners.

What condition must men fulfill if they would participate in the new birth? They must *believe*. This was hinted in verse 12, but is now made explicit (vs. 15). This is no momentary attraction but an irrevocable decision to depend only and forever upon the Saviour.

26

It is possible that verses 16-21 are contributed by John rather than Jesus. Nicodemus seems to fade from view here. He is no longer addressed. Every man takes his place.

The miniature gospel, as it has been called (vs. 16) is not merely a summary of preceding statements. New elements are the love of God for the world and the issue of that love in the gift of His Son. *Only begotten* is the translation of *monogenēs,* which means one of a kind. God had only one Son bearing His perfect likeness. Him He did not spare, but delivered Him up for us all (Rom. 8:32). *Whosoever* opens the door of salvation for all classes and conditions of men. Nicodemus' possession of religion would not admit him, nor could the sinfulness of the Samaritan woman exclude her (Chapter 4). God is rich unto all that call upon Him.

Plain indeed is the destiny of those who will not believe, but the primary purpose of Christ's coming was not to judge but to provide salvation (vs. 17). The believer escapes judgment for his sins and for no other reason than that those sins have been assumed for him by Christ. The rejector of Christ stands under judgment, in advance of the final assize, for the reason that he repudiates the only cure for sins. A person's moral aim has much to do with faith or unbelief. If there is a love of sin, there will inevitably be a dislike of anything that means rebuke of that sin. On the other hand, if one responds to the light of revelation in Christ, it is an indication that he desires to walk in that light and

27

live a life pleasing to God. Such a man has already begun to work the works of God (vs. 21; cf. 6:29).

6. The Final Witness of John the Baptist to Jesus (3:22-36). It seems that for a time after Jesus began His public ministry, John continued his work along the lines which had characterized it from the beginning. The evangelist presumably includes this section in his Gospel in order to make clear that John was not in competition with the Christ. Both were baptizing, but in different areas: Jesus in Judea, John farther north along the Jordan River near Salim. Jesus directed the work of His disciples, but did not Himself baptize (see 4:2; cf. I Cor. 1:13-17).

All this baptizing activity led to reflection in some quarters as to the meaning of this in relation to Jewish purification laws and customs (cf. 2:6). A Jew (so the best text reads in 3:25) engaged some of John's disciples in discussion on this point. This led in turn to an inquiring protest by these men to their own leader concerning Jesus' growing popularity. They resented it, yet realized that John had contributed to Jesus' following by bearing witness to Him (vs. 26).

In this delicate situation John showed his true greatness of spirit. He reminded his disciples that he was not the Christ but the forerunner, and this by divine appointment (vss. 27-28). He could no more feel resentment at Jesus' success than could a friend of the bridegroom at the latter's marriage (vs. 29). His own following must decrease as that of Jesus increases (he had already contributed several disciples; cf. 1:35-51).

In the remainder of the chapter John says nothing further about himself. Some students have concluded from this that these are the words of the evangelist but this cannot be certainly demonstrated. John was aware of the heavenly origin of the One greater than himself (cf. 3:13; cf. 8:23) and of his own earthly origin and nature (vs. 31). The Lord from Heaven had brought with Him the experience of Heaven's reality, yet earthlings had turned a deaf ear to His testimony (vs. 32; cf. 3:11). The rejection was general yet there were exceptions who saw truth in Jesus and believed that God had sent Him (vs. 33; cf. 1:11, 12). They perceived that God's Spirit was at work in Him, not in a limited degree, as in the prophets, but *without measure* (vs. 34). In addition to a fully authenticated teaching ministry, Jesus had another yet to be exercised, in the main. He is the appointed Judge of all. He who rejects the Son rejects the Father. By rejecting the one whom the Father loves he brings upon himself the wrath of God (vss. 35-36). This truth has been stated in similar language in 3:16-18.

7. The witness in Samaria (4:1-42). Opposition by the Pharisees to Jesus on the basis of His growing strength is given as the reason for the Lord's decision to leave Judea in favor of Galilee, where their opposition would count for less. The decision dictated a journey through Samaria, which was the normal route when time was at all a factor. These bits of information (vss. 1-4) prepare the reader for the account of the ministry in Samaria, which is divided into the two episodes of Jesus' conversation with the woman at the well (vss. 5-26) and the contact with the men of Samaria (vss. 27-42).

There is a strong possibility that the town near which the well was located was Shechem rather than Sychar. Archeological research points in this direction, and manuscript authority for the name is not lacking. In the patriarchal age, when the country was just being developed, many wells were dug. Jacob's well may still be seen, an excavation some 75 feet deep. It made a natural stopping place for Jesus, who by this time was exhausted from travel and needed refreshment. The sixth hour is usually taken to be noon, though it may possibly be six in the evening. Left alone there in His weariness, Jesus awaited the return of the disciples who had gone into the town to buy food. Before they arrived, a woman of Samaria approached to draw water, and of her the Lord requested a drink.

Samaritans were suspicious of Jews. Bad feeling had existed between them ever since those Jews who returned from captivity refused to permit the Samaritan people to share in the rebuilding of the temple at Jerusalem. It strikes this woman as strange that the Jew before her makes such a request. It pleases her momentarily that she has the upper hand. But she is curious at Jesus' readiness to break the barrier of hostility and custom. Her surprise becomes still more pointed if we follow David Daube's suggestion regarding the last part of verse 9, reading it thus: "Jews do not use vessels together with Samaritans" (*The New Testament and Rabbinic Judaism,* Athlone Press, University of

30

London, 1956, pp. 375-379). That Jews avoided all dealings with Samaritans is contradicted by the shopping expedition of the disciples. The next words of Jesus are sufficient to shake her condescension. There are things she does not know—the gift of God, even living water, dispensed from the Son of God, who is the source of life (cf. 7:37-39). Unable to think except in materialistic terms, the woman glances at the empty hands of the stranger and then at the well, where the water line stood far below the surface. How could He offer her living water such as bubbled up from the spring at the bottom of the well?

But Jesus' thoughts were not on anything earthly, but on a provision for the soul's deep thirst that nothing material can satisfy. He tried to explain that He could plant a fountain of eternal life in the woman's heart (vs. 14), but all she could picture was a constant supply of the same thing she was getting from day to day, only mysteriously and perhaps magically produced. She soon discovered there was a price to pay. Her past life must be set before her as an open book to show her how great is her need of cleansing. Fascinated by Jesus' words and manner, she is ready to talk to Him about the intimate things of her life, confessing that she has no husband. Her wonder grows as the Lord details her present and past relationships with men, six of them in all. The very number of the marriages suggests the ease with which some of them were dissolved in favor of others, until finally the formality of a wedding was dispensed with entirely. The woman was a self-confessed sinner.

31

This exposure came by a simple statement of fact. Jesus did not go into embarrassing details, nor did he berate her for her sin. As a result, she was able to look away from herself, since no defense of her past was provoked through censure, and marvel at the One before her. Who could He be? Could He—yes, He must be— a prophet who knew what others did without observing them (II Kings 5:25-27). Perhaps, then, He could direct her poor, confused soul so that she could get right with God. What was the correct approach? Were the Jews right in insisting one must go to Jerusalem and worship, and so find God? Her Samaritan ancestors had laid down a similar claim for their local shrine at Mount Gerizim. She knew that the place of worship, where priests minister in the name of God, is the place to find forgiveness. What she did not know was that Jesus is prophet and priest in one, able to disclose sin and also to forgive.

The Lord took advantage of the woman's question to make a notable pronouncement on worship (vss. 21-24). It was in part a corrective statement. Samaritan worship was as confused and commingled as their racial stock (II Kings 17:24-41). The Jews had a clear revelation from God and were no longer guilty of idolatry. Salvation was to be found among them as the covenant people of God. However, even Jewish worship was limited. An *hour* was coming (recall how often this word is used of Jesus' death) when even Jerusalem would cease to be the place where God placed His name in an exclusive sense. The veil would soon be rent, then city and temple would be shattered,

32

teaching men that they could have access to the Father anywhere, as long as they came to Him in the right way—in spirit and in truth. The meaning of those words is not exhausted by conceiving of worship as freed of local and ceremonial encumbrances which a more refined view of God makes possible. Everything depends on the coming hour, which is present in the sense that the Redeemer is here and His reconciling work is as good as done. Spiritual worship is only possible through the Spirit who makes acceptable the approach of believers to God through Christ (Phil. 3:3; I Pet. 2:5). When the Spirit controls, error vanishes. He is the Spirit of truth, who makes possible the vision of God as He is—Spirit. The ministry of both the Son (cf. 1:18) and the Spirit conspire to make the Father a reality.

Jesus' revelation of true worship includes the gratifying assurance that the Father seeks true worshipers. This was an encouragement to the Samaritan woman who may well have felt that she did not qualify because of her mongrel religion as well as her misspent life.

The Samaritans, like the Jews, had a Messianic hope. But like Martha's concept of the resurrection, it was remote. How electrifying to hear Jesus of Nazareth say, *I that speak unto thee am he!* There is no need for wistful longing, but a call for immediate faith.

By this time the disciples arrived and by their coming terminated the conversation. But the woman had heard enough. She left her waterpot, a pledge that she would return, but even more significant as indicating that she was beginning to drink of the promised living water.

Even as Christ had lost for the time the desire for food in the consuming joy of pointing a needy soul to the place of forgiveness and rest, so could the woman forget physical thirst as the fountain of new life surged up within her.

.Her report to the men of the city advised them that she had met a man who told her all things she had done (vs. 29). It was a dogma of her faith that the coming Messiah would tell *all things* (vs. 25). This man had done that as far as she was concerned. Could He be any other than the Christ? By phrasing it as she did she was able to plant an idea without appearing to teach the men, who would resent any such attempt. Her face must have reflected her inner conviction. Instead of the one man she had been asked to bring, a whole company of men made their way out of the city to confront Jesus for themselves.

While this was going on, the disciples were getting some instruction from the Master. They had started the conversation on the theme of food (vs. 31). He neatly turned it in the direction of spiritual sowing and reaping. In the physical, there is a *four months* interval between sowing and reaping. He Himself has been busy sowing seed that afternoon, and now look!—the harvest already appears. The eyes of the disciples were lifted up to follow His as He gazed along the path to the city, which was now filled by a throng of men coming to meet Him. What a harvest—ripe, ready, rewarding! It has required more than one laborer. Jesus planted the seed in the woman's heart, then she bore her testimony and others responded. This is the pattern the disciples will follow. Sometimes they will sow, at other times they will reap the harvest that others have sown (vss. 36-38).

The Samaritan incident closes on a very human note. Many who believed let the woman know that the real factor in their conversion was not her testimony but their own contact with the Lord. They were unwilling to concede to her any superior advantage. But all were agreed that their spiritual provincialism was over. They had come to know the Saviour of the world (vs. 42).

8. The Witness in Galilee through the Healing of the Official's Son (4:43-54). After two days in Samaria the Lord and His disciples continued on to Galilee. The reason for this visit was put in proverbial terms by Jesus. A prophet has no honor in his own country. In the Synoptics the saying is applied to Nazareth (Matt. 13:57). Here it seems to refer to Galilee as a whole. He had been favorably received in Judea except by the rulers, and His reason for departing into Galilee was simply their opposition (cf. vs. 1). It is possible, however, that the proverb is differently applied in this Gospel, where Jesus' own country may refer to Judea as the main center of His ministry, in which case emphasis should be given to the hearty reception extended to Him by the Galileans (vs. 45) in contrast to the coolness of official Judaism toward Him.

The only incident of this Galilean visit reported by John concerns the nobleman of Capernaum, whose son lay gravely ill. Perhaps the father's resort to Jesus was prompted by the reports of His miracles brought back from Jerusalem by people from this section (vs. 45). Journeying to Cana, he implored the Saviour to come and give His help. Having had experience of "miracle believers" (2:23-25), Jesus momentarily classes this man with such, to test him (vs. 48). But as it turned out, the father was prepared to believe Jesus' word that his request had been granted. Only later did he have corroboration from his servants. There was no question about the miracle, since the fever relaxed its hold at the very time Jesus had spoken (vs. 53). The whole household was impressed, and as a result believed. Miracles have a place in creating the response of faith (14:11; 20:31), provided faith looks on from the sign to the Saviour Himself.

9. The witness in the Healing of the Impotent Man (5:1-16). The Jews observed several annual feasts or festivals. It is unlikely that this is Passover, which is elsewhere explicitly designated (2:23; 6:4; 13:1). The city Jerusalem was more crowded than usual at festival time. But the reader's attention is directed to a *multitude* of a special sort—the maimed and decrepit who waited hopefully in the porticoes of the pool of Bethesda. A spot answering well to the description given here has been excavated a short distance north of the temple area. This crowd of unfortunates was lured to this spot by the reputation of the pool. It was thought that an angel periodically troubled the water, and the first person to reach the water thereafter would be healed. The last clause of verse 3 and all of verse 4 is absent from the best manuscripts, but this portion undoubtedly gives a correct summary of the popular ideas relative to the pool.

One man, crippled for nearly forty years, drew Jesus' special consideration. If it seems strange that the Lord would ask a man whether or not he wanted to be whole, one need only reflect that some sick and infirm people really prefer their state, since it wins them sympathy and aid. But this man confessed his helplessness and repeated disappointment *(I have no man)*. He was to find immediately that he did have a Friend, after all, whose help would make descent into the pool unnecessary. Obeying Jesus' command to rise, the impotent man found that when the Lord commands He also supplies the means for complying with the command (cf. Acts 3:6-8). He was able to stand, and to walk, and also to carry his bed (a mattress or pallet). A sort of postscript to the account of the miracle adds the fact that this was done on *the Sabbath* (vs. 9). The deed would be counted by the Jews as work, a violation of Sabbath rest. This circumstance made a collision between Jesus and the Jewish leaders inevitable. At first the healed man was blamed, but when it appeared that the responsibility really lay with Jesus, He became the target of attack. It should be noted that Jesus did not try to avoid giving aid because it was the Sabbath. He took the initiative, rather than the infirm man. Even then, He deliberately made himself known to the man afterward, in the temple, so that the information would be bound to reach the authorities that He, rather than some other, had done this thing.

To Jesus, such a use of the Sabbath was thoroughly

defensible, not only from the standpoint of the deed of mercy accomplished but also from His own standpoint as Lord of the Sabbath, able to use the day as He saw fit.

The Lord's search for the man in the temple, where he had gone to give thanks for his cure, shows that the miracle was not done to enhance His reputation. He had the welfare of the individual at heart. Bodily soundness was not enough. What about the sin problem? The presumption here is that forgiveness of sins was granted (cf. Mk. 2:5-12). Restored physical powers might prompt the man to indulge in sin which his former incapacity made difficult. Against this Jesus warns solemnly (vs. 14). There is forgiveness with God that He may be feared.

Armed with knowledge that Jesus was responsible for this Sabbath deed, the Jews sought to put Him to death. He was a dangerous lawbreaker, as they saw it. They had offered the cripple nothing but neglect, but now that he was well, instead of rejoicing in his deliverance, they planned to kill his benefactor (vs. 16).

10. The Witness of Jesus' Authority (5:17-47). It is noteworthy that in His discussion with the Jews over this incident, Jesus did not argue the question of Sabbath violation (cf. 7:23) but lifted the issue to a higher level, namely, His authority as the Son of God. As such, He was a rightful collaborator with the Father (literally, His own Father, vs. 18). This was rejected as rank blasphemy, making Him doubly liable to death. In the eyes of the Jews a mere man was making himself out to be God. But one who would do that was simply filled with arrogance, whereas the next words reveal the real spirit of the Speaker. He can do nothing alone, and what He performs is a result of seeing the Father at work (vs. 19). Such humility and dependence do not belong to a Messianic pretender. The relation between Father and Son is one of love and confidence. Much is therefore given to the Son to do. Greater works can be expected. An example is the raising of the dead, not one only, but the dead as a whole.

Another greater work is *judgment* (vs. 22). Clearly the function of judgment belongs only to God in the ultimate sense. That He would commit it to the Son is evidence of the equality of the Son with the Father. Again the claim is universal—*all* judgment. In that day, if not before, all who honor the Father will be constrained to do the same for the Son. Faith in the Son cannot be separated from faith in the One who sent Him (vs. 24). Every true believer will escape the judgment visited on other men for their sins.

Jesus returns to the theme of resurrection for a more complete statement, but not to the neglect of judgment (vss. 25-29). This fact underscores the closeness of relationship between these two features of the end time. As in the teaching about worship (cf. 4:21, 23) the *hour* of realization is *coming,* but it has an anticipation in the present *(now is).* Those who are dead in sins, unresponsive to God, are being exposed to the voice of Christ. Those who hear in faith become spiritually alive now (vs. 25). This means a sharing in the very life of Father and Son (vs. 26).

Bodily resurrection awaits a future day. Two classes of men will participate and the results will be identical with the verdict reached upon men here and now in accordance with their attitude toward Christ. It will be either *life* or *judgment* (vs. 29; cf. 5:24; 3:36). To do good includes the exercise of faith (cf. 6:29); to do evil includes the rejection of God's provision in the Son (cf. 3:19-20).

Returning to the charge of blasphemy, Jesus defends Himself on the ground that He is not bearing witness about Himself. Jewish law required two witnesses. To His own claims the Father bears attestation (vss. 30-32). The witness of John the Baptist, given at some length in the early chapters of this Gospel, was helpful, and many Jews were impressed, but Jesus Himself relies on the *greater witness* of the Father. The proof of the Father's endorsement is to be found, for those who need "evidence," in the works the Father has given Him to do.

If it be objected that men cannot see God and therefore cannot be expected to recognize one who comes claiming to be His Son, this difficulty is overcome by the record God has given in the Old Testament Scriptures, so that one should be able to recognize Him if he has read the record with care. This is the great tragedy of Judaism. It has searched the Scriptures and has failed to find the life there promised because it has refused to recognize in Jesus the fulfillment of prophecy. Ironically the Jews are ready to prefer a pretender to Him who comes in the Father's name (vs. 43). So the Scriptures are an added witness to Jesus. He affirms the

40

validity of Messianic prophecy. Since Moses was so highly venerated by the Jews, Jesus deliberately limits the authentication of Himself to the Torah, the five books of Moses. One of the clearest references is Deuteronomy 18:15-18.

11. The Witness of the Bread of Life (6:1-71). Again Jesus is back in Galilee, and once more His miracles of healing make their appeal, so that a great company of people followed Him and His disciples when He moved toward the eastern side of the sea of Galilee (vss. 1-4). Being Passover time, there was a heavy spring growth of grass (cf. vss. 4, 10). This time notice may explain, in part, the presence of the multitude, since many pilgrims on their way to the feast were glad for the opportunity of contact with Jesus.

But the multitude created a problem. How were they to be fed? Philip estimated that it would take a day's pay of two hundred laborers to buy sufficient bread. Probably the treasury of the apostolic band did not contain that amount, so nothing was done. Furthermore, bread could not be purchased in this region away from the cities. Andrew volunteered the information that a boy had presented himself, having five small loaves made of barley meal and two small fish. Andrew himself viewed the supply as hopelessly inadequate. Nevertheless Jesus proceeded with preparations for ministering to the multitude. Order was essential. The people must be seated in groups, permitting the passage between them of those who would serve (cf. Mark

6:39). After a word of thanks to God, the breaking of the bread and fish and their distribution began. Miraculously the meager provision was multiplied in the process of distribution, till all were fed and satisfied and the fragments gathered up. Each disciple was able to bring back to Jesus a basketful. The generosity of grace does not encourage wastefulness of what God bestows.

The miracle, instead of making the crowd restful and content, awakened in them the stirrings of a tremendous enthusiasm. Jesus loomed in their eyes as the promised *prophet* (Deut. 18:15-18). Excitement mounted as they agreed that they should draft the Nazarene as *king.* If He could solve their food problem, why not their other problems as well, including the recapture of their independence as a nation? But Jesus' kingdom was not based on such considerations (cf. 18:36). He could no more permit Himself to be taken by force for this purpose than to be made a captive of the Jewish leaders before His time (vs. 15; cf. 10:39).

After the miracle, the disciples took ship for Capernaum and were well out into the big lake when a storm threatened them. This was one of the few occasions when they were separated from the Master. They needed Him desperately now. Unexpectedly He came and brought them safely to the farther shore (cf. Ps. 107:23-30). The Lord who works for the good of the multitude may be expected to intervene on behalf of His own.

On the next day the crowd, not easily shaken off, caught up with Jesus in Capernaum. He showed His displeasure with them by uncovering the real motive for their interest in Him. It was a materialistic desire to have a convenient provider. They did not regard His miracles (signs) in their true significance as pointers to spiritual truth (vs. 26). The Lord's word provoked two questions. Since He had commanded them to labor, what were they to do that would satisfy God (vs. 28)? The answer was unexpected—believe in the One God has sent. Jesus had rebuked them on the signs. Now they demanded a sign which would compel their faith in Him. Could He match the miracle of the wilderness wanderings, when bread was supplied from Heaven (suggesting that Jesus' miracle of the loaves was a mere earthly performance)? He sensed an unfavorable comparison with Moses, so it was necessary to state that the bread came not from Moses but from God, who had now given *the true bread* from Heaven (vs. 32). The true in this Gospel means the ideal, the ultimately efficacious. Why was Jesus the true bread? Because He could do more than fill empty stomachs. He came down from Heaven to give life to the world. Still thinking on a physical level, the people are eager for this bread (vs. 34; cf. 4:15). It was time to make the nature of the heavenly bread so clear that none could mistake it (vs. 35). Christ identifies Himself with the bread of life. Faith in Him brings abiding satisfaction—an end to man's spiritual quest (cf. 4:14). His leaving the scene of the miracle must not be viewed as indifference toward men. On the contrary, He stands ready to receive all who come to Him (vs. 37; cf. Matt. 11:28). Even if this were not His own

43

desire, it is the will of the Father that none who is given to the Son (cf. 17:6, 9) be lost. This was a far superior credential to any Moses had, for he saw a nation defect and perish. Resurrection will prove to be the final chapter in the saving process entrusted to Jesus (vs. 39).

This exalted teaching met opposition (vss. 41-42). How could one whose parents were known to these Galileans be from Heaven? This was a stumbling-block to faith. The truth of John 1:18 had not been grasped.

Jesus acknowledged the difficulty which His humanity posed, but indicated that it was overcome by a divine provision: the supernatural inclination to turn to Him (Christ) put in the heart of all who truly knew the Father and were open to His direction (vss. 43-46).

Then He pressed once more His claim to be the giver of spiritual life (vss. 47-51). Heavenly manna such as ancient Israel knew lacked any such power. The fathers died physically. Jesus as the bread of life guarantees freedom from spiritual death. But the point of release of the bread had not yet come. It would come with the giving of His *body*. The saying strongly reminds one of Jesus' words at the Last Supper.

Still blinded by their materialistic outlook, the people express to one another their incredulity. How can this be (vs. 52; cf. 3:9)? Such language suggested cannibalism. To make matters worse, Jesus added the necessity of drinking His blood (vs. 53). Taken literally, this would violate the Law (Lev. 17:10-14). The people were stunned.

Unabashed, the Lord repeated the necessity of partaking of His flesh and blood, adding that thereby a community of life would be set up between Him and those who fulfilled His conditions (vs. 56). And then with one sentence He lifted the whole matter onto a plane where none should be confused or offended (vs. 57). If He Himself lived by the Father (and surely there was nothing physical about that arrangement), neither is there anything physical in the requirement that one must eat of the Saviour in order to live by means of Him. Food is a means of sustaining life as it is assimilated into the body; even so it is possible to appropriate Christ by faith and so live unto God.

The final reaction of the audience, despite the marvelous words of Jesus, was negative. They were still offended. The teaching about Jesus' flesh and blood was counted a *hard saying* (vs. 60). He responded by noting that more supernatural demonstrations were to come. What will they think when the Son of Man returns to Heaven? Have the words of Jesus offended? This is strange, for they are spirit and life. They communicate real blessing. They are not empty promises (cf. vs. 68).

With the conclusion of the discourse, *many* who had thought of themselves as Jesus' disciples found they had come to the parting of the ways. They *walked no more with him* (vs. 66).

The defection was so general that it threatened to become complete. Would the Twelve join the exodus?

45

Jesus gave them the opportunity. One of that company could not understand why Jesus had refused to be made a king, and he was just as offended as the multitude over this talk about eating the flesh and drinking the blood of the Son of Man. But he was ashamed to depart. So he would stay and betray (vs. 71). Another disciple must have had some doubts and perplexities, but when faced with the option of deserting Jesus or remaining, despite his misgivings, he knew he must stay. No other than Jesus had the words of eternal life (vs. 68). The one who was to deny the Saviour was poles apart from the betrayer, both now and in the dark hours of that last night before the Lord suffered.

12. The Witness at the Feast of Tabernacles (7: 1-53). From the opening words it is probable that a period of ministry in Judea is left unreported beyond the observation that it stirred up further opposition from the Jewish leaders. Jesus then returned to Galilee.

Tabernacles was a well-attended Jewish festival, observed in the month of October. The word used here means the building of tents or booths. As far as possible people resided in booths made from branches of trees, in order to memorialize the nation's manner of life when they came out of Egypt (Lev. 23:39-43). Jesus' brothers pressed Him to attend this festival on the ground that He would have a large number of people to witness His mighty deeds (vs. 3). Who were the *disciples* mentioned here? Jesus' Galilean following had largely deserted Him (6:66). Yet there were others from Galilee who could be strengthened in their attachment by a strong demonstration of His power (cf. 4:45). Perhaps Jesus' Judean admirers are in view here also. The brothers advised Him to be bolder, to call attention to Himself in public. He needed to promote Himself (vs. 4). Such suggestions were in line with their unsaved condition (cf. vs. 5). Jesus intimates that when His hour (death) comes, He will be in the public eye, but not in such a way as to receive the plaudits of the world. Rather He will draw down upon Himself the hatred of men for exposing the iniquity of their works (vss. 6-9).

When He finally went up to the festival Jesus went, as it were, *in secret*. This does not mean that He went incognito or that He remained hidden (cf. vss. 14, 26). It means rather that He went without any attempt at public display such as the brothers suggested. Before His arrival He was the topic of conversation among the people. They sensed the tension between Him and the leaders and wondered if He would dare to show Himself (vss. 10-13).

Jesus a controversial figure (vss. 14-53). After a delay of half a week, Jesus appeared at the temple and, as usual, began to teach. Those who heard marveled, not because He was uneducated, but because He lacked technical training such as the rabbis received. The people did not think of Him as a man of letters, literate in the Law of Moses. But He had something better than a scribal training, for God, in sending Him, gave Him the message (cf. Deut. 18:15-18). If anyone makes the divine will his desire and choice (as Jesus Himself had done), he will not have much trouble deciding whether Jesus is a fraud or one sent from Heaven (vs. 17). One of our Lord's credentials is His concern for the glory of God rather than His own (vs. 18). The Jewish leaders might profess to be seeking God's glory, but a practical test proved otherwise. They gloried in Moses and in the Law he had left for them, yet they demonstrated their unrighteousness by breaking the Law. Their very attempt to kill Jesus was murder, a breach of the sixth commandment (vs. 19, cf. 5:16, 18).

Knowing that His healing of the impotent man on the Sabbath rankled in the minds of the Jews, Jesus brings the matter to the fore once again, in such a way as to relate it to the Law (vss. 21-24). Moses laid down the duty of Sabbath observance, to be sure, but he also legislated circumcision on the eighth day (Lev. 12:3). If the eighth day fell on a Sabbath, the duty of circumcision (which involved work) took precedence over the duty of Sabbath rest. Surely the renovation of a man was as important as the fulfilling of a ceremony. The Jews were seemingly showing themselves incapable of right judgment (vs. 24, cf. vs. 18).

These remarks stirred up discussion about the central issue—the person, the office, and the authority of this Galilean Teacher (vss. 25-31). Local residents, who knew well the animosity of their rulers toward Jesus, found it hard to understand how they would permit Him to speak so boldly in public. It almost seemed as though they were changing their minds and inclining to the view that this prophet was indeed the Messiah (vss. 25-26). Yet this was incredible, because even they, the unlearned, realized that Jesus could not be the Messiah. They knew His background, and the rulers knew it too. He lacked the mystery which the true Messiah would have (cf. Matt. 24:23-25). Perhaps this reflects the influence of Jewish apocalyptic writings which pictured the Messiah as a heavenly figure who would suddenly come to the help of His people.

Jesus cannot permit Himself to be dismissed in this offhand fashion. His reply emphasizes that what they know of His earthly life is true, but they are ignorant of His heavenly origin, and this ignorance reveals their ignorance of God, who had sent Him (vs. 28). This caused offense and there was a rush to take Him, but it evaporated into helplessness. It may have been this circumstance, added to the miracles of previous days, that constrained some of the people to the opinion that no claimant to the office of Messiah could do more than this one (vs. 31). There is nothing to indicate that this show of faith was any more genuine than previous instances (cf. 2:23-25). Nevertheless it prodded the authorities to take action. Officers were dispatched to arrest Jesus (vs. 32).

Meanwhile the Lord continued His teaching. Some are seeking Him because of the glamor of the miracles. Others are seeking Him to take His life. The latter group will succeed, but only when the hour for His departure (death, etc.) has come. After that it will be futile to seek Him, whether under pressure of burdens imposed by religious leaders or trials occasioned by national disaster. Now is their day of salvation, if they will embrace it. The talk about departure brought on speculation that Jesus was contemplating a withdrawal from Palestine to the Jews of the Dispersion, where He would also find Gentiles (in the synagogues). The people did not realize that the Lord would return to the Father.

To be added to His other credentials—sent of God, seeking the glory of God, and then returning to God—is the high prerogative of supplying the Spirit (vss. 37-39). The occasion of this claim was the termination of the feast. Day by day, as a part of the celebration of the preservation of Israel in the wilderness wanderings, a bowl of water had been brought from the pool of Siloam into the temple, recalling the supply of water from the rock (Exodus 17). In the very repetition lay the confession of incompleteness (cf. Heb. 10:1, 2). Did the thirst remain? One offered satisfaction—*come unto me and drink* (cf. 4:14; Matt. 11:28). There is promise of more than personal satisfaction. The refreshed soul becomes a channel of blessing to others. No certain passage of *Scripture* has been identified as being in the mind of Jesus. Perhaps He is using *Scripture* in a collective sense—the consensus of several passages. This fullness, John adds, is due to the Spirit, whose coming into the lives of God's people in the special and intimate way pictured here awaited the completion of Jesus' work on earth and His glorification (cf. 16:7-14).

The words of Jesus set off a wave of popular speculation (vss. 40-44). To some He was the prophet (Deut. 18:15-18), to others the Messiah. Still others objected to this identification on the basis of Jesus' Galilean origin (not realizing He had been born in Bethlehem as the Micah prophecy necessitated). A group shared the position of the authorities that Jesus was an annoying pretender and deceiver. They would like to have apprehended Him, but were frustrated. Another group—the officers sent by the hierarchy—who arrived at about this time, was equally unsuccessful, but for a different reason. They were overawed by the words of Jesus, and the manner. *Never man spake like this man*—such exalted claims balanced by such deep humility.

Annoyed at their failure to get Jesus in their grasp and angered at the popular support He had gained under their very noses, the Pharisees vented their scorn for the rabble—the common people that did not know the Law (vs. 49). Nicodemus ventured to suggest that knowledge of the Law, if it was thorough, would not lead their body (the Sanhedrin) to judge a man without a fair hearing and a careful scrutinizing of his works (vs. 51). This complaint stung the rest. Had Nicodemus become pro-Galilean? Galilee furnished no prophet. Jesus could be no exception. One recently discovered Greek manuscript has *the* prophet here, a reading which may have originated in the realization that Galilee had furnished Jonah and that the debate here was over *the* prophet (cf. vs. 40). This incident is a steppingstone between Nicodemus as an inquirer (chapter 3) and as a bold supporter and friend of Jesus (19:39-42).

13. The Witness of a Loving and Forgiving Saviour (8:1-11). This portion is lacking in the leading manuscripts of John. Doubtless it is a faithful record of an event in the life of our Lord, though not a part of the Gospel as originally written.

Failing to take Jesus by force, the scribes and Pharisees tried a more subtle approach. They would discredit Him in the eyes of the people. Their manner was rude —interrupting the Lord as He taught, by dragging a woman taken in adultery into His presence. They had no more concern for her feelings than for His. Their motive was to get a basis of accusation against Him (vs. 6). Their method was to pit His well-known love and friendship for sinners over against the sternness of the Mosaic Law which called for stoning in such cases.

In His own manner, Jesus matched their rudeness with deliberate preoccupation, as He wrote on the ground. He was ignoring them as a rebuke to their harsh spirit. In His method, He contrived to embarrass the intruders, turning the tables on them. Through it all He had in view an educative motive, showing that the touching of the conscience of men was more potent than the debating of the requirements of the Law. The accusers went out as accused—the self-accused. This was a far greater victory for righteousness than the sanctioning of the penalty against the woman.

Jesus' manner with the woman was one of gentleness. His method was a refusal to condemn her, knowing that she did not need that, since her own heart condemned her. Yet He did not exonerate her or condone

52

her sin. His motive was to assure her of forgiveness and grant her a passport to a new and better life.

14. **The Witness of the "I Am"** (8:12-59). Here the Jews asked our Lord a total of seven questions, the crucial one being, "Who art thou?" (vs. 25). His final reply asserted equality with the self-revealing God of the Old Testament—"I Am" (vs. 58).

The passage begins as well as ends with an "I Am," (vs. 12) and includes many in between (vss. 16, 18, 23, 24, 28). Proud of their enlightened leadership, the Pharisees deplored the unwillingness of the common people to follow them (7:48-49). But they were blind leaders of the blind. Jesus alone has *the light of life* (vs. 12; cf. 1:4). He is able to light the path to glory for all in the world who will follow Him. It was of no avail to challenge this great assertion (vs. 13), for it was no wild, fantastic boast. The speaker knew well His heavenly origin and His heavenly destination (vs. 14). This simple fact meant that His claims and judgments were backed by the heavenly Father (vss. 16-18). Jesus' opponents demand that He produce His Father (would they spell it as father?). The rest of the chapter is a discussion of parentage, of pedigree—that of Jesus and that of the Jewish leaders. It is no wonder that the latter are ignorant of the Father, seeing they have not come to know the Son, though He is in their midst as sent of God (vs. 19).

Time is running out. Whether the Jews seek Jesus, after He goes His way, out of curiosity or despair amid their calamities, He will not be available (vs. 21; cf.

7:34). This time (contrast 7:35) the Jews surmise that He will resort to suicide. They are only right to the extent that there will be a death; it will not be self-inflicted. Through a death imposed by men and yet determined by God—and accepted by Himself, He will leave the world to return whence He has come, manifesting His utter dissimilarity to His murderers. God will receive Him even if they have failed to do so (vs. 23). It is high time they consider their own death, which will be a hopeless one unless they trust Him, for He alone has the cure for their sins (vs. 24).

Now comes the pointed question, "Who art thou?" Jesus is an enigma to those who refuse to see Him in the light of revelation as the Son of God. What is needed is not more revelation (vs. 25) but a little faith. If His hearers have refused the light, to grant more would only increase the condemnation (vs. 26). The future will vindicate Him—His return to the Father by way of the Cross, as this is preached with power by His witnesses after the ascension (vs. 28). To please the Father, whether in life or death (*always*) is the Son's delight (cf. II Cor. 5:9, A.S.V.). This selflessness seemed to make an impression on many who heard Him (vs. 30).

Once again, the faith was inadequate. This time the "believers" demonstrated their unwillingness to *continue* in Jesus' word as He began to unfold it (vs. 31). Faith is the key to truth, and truth brings freedom. One is no longer bound hopelessly in sin and superstition and obedience to a false leadership. Proud of their history as the covenant people of God, the Jews grew indignant at the suggestion that they had not attained freedom. They overlooked their bondage to sin. Only the Son can bring deliverance from its yoke (vs. 36).

The Jews had put forward their relation to Abraham as the basis for the claim that they were free. They were of the chosen race (vs. 33). Jesus acknowledges the relationship (vs. 37), but not the assumption based on it. The Jews felt that to be descended from Abraham made them accepted with God. But Jesus showed them that they were not walking in the steps of Abraham, and offered their murderous attitude toward Himself as proof.

At this point the Jews assume a superior air. Why should they not glory in their Abrahamic descent? That is more than He can do. The implication is that Jesus was born of fornication, for the *we* is emphatic (vs. 41). It seems that this slander was invented at an early time. It is reflected also in Matthew's account of the birth of Jesus, where he undertakes to show the true state of affairs.

After such a charge, the exchange between Jesus and the Jews becomes more virulent. He asserts that their real father is the Devil. Consequently they are found doing his works rather than Abraham's. The Devil branded himself from the beginning as a *liar* (his misrepresentation to Eve, Gen. 3:1-5) and a *murderer* (Adam and his posterity received the sentence of death because of his enticement to sin). Actual murder is traced to the evil one in I John 3:12.

In contrast to the Devil, Jesus speaks the truth. His

hearers show their Satanic affiliation by refusing the truth. They show they are not of God (vss. 45-47). Relationship is still the burden of the argument. The Jews reveal their malice by suggesting that Jesus, rather than they themselves, has association with the Devil (by having a demon within him) and that He is a Samaritan, by which they probably have in mind the mixed blood of this race, and so are reviving the slur on His origin (cf. vs. 41).

Once more Jesus warns that to dishonor and reject Him is only to invite divine judgment (vss. 49-50). But to receive Him and follow His word means the avoidance of judgment. Such a one shall never see death (cf. 11:25). Writing this off as ridiculous, as evidence that He was possessed, the Jews think to dispute Jesus by showing that death has claimed the holy men of the past, including Abraham (vs. 52). Still rating Jesus as a mere man, they ask incredulously whether He considers Himself greater than Abraham (vs. 53).

Jesus prefers not to say anything that could be construed as an attempt at self-glorification. He can rest content in the knowledge that the Father honors Him (vs. 54). But since Abraham has been brought into the conversation, He must place Himself and Abraham in proper perspective. The patriarch, so honored by the Jews, looked forward longingly to Christ and His day. To think that his descendants were seeing that day with their own eyes and yet were despising what Abraham rejoiced in!

Unable to follow these exalted lines of thought, the

Jews found fresh ground for scorn in the assertion of Jesus' connection with Abraham. Had he seen Abraham (putting the matter this way suggested Abraham's superiority to Jesus)? The answer was monumental. *Before Abraham was, I am* (cf. 1:3, 30). This was the language by which Jehovah God revealed Himself (Ex. 3:14). The one whom they dubbed a demon-possessed man of dubious origin asserts that He is the eternal God. No issue could be more sharply drawn.

15. The Witness of the Light of the World (9: 1-41). Jesus' previous affirmation (8:12) now takes on concrete meaning. The case of the blind man was particularly hopeless from the human standpoint— blind from birth (cf. vs. 32). Jesus' disciples, like the friends of Job, assume that any striking misfortune must be traced to sin. How strange that they should attribute this man's affliction to his own sin, which would require the sin to have occurred before birth, that is, in a previous existence. For this Scripture teaching affords no basis.

Jesus lifted the matter at once to an infinitely higher plane, indicating that the affliction was intended to minister to the glory of God (vs. 3). Instantly the misfortune comes into new focus. It looms as a privilege, not a burden.

Swiftly the Master Workman addressed Himself to the work (cf. 5:17) of admitting light where darkness had reigned so long. Yet the cure is not effected immediately, but in such a way as to test the man's faith.

The scene recalls the creation in two respects. As man was formed from the ground, this material is now used again for reconstruction. Further, as the Creator had said, "Let there be light," so in effect He now issues that command again. The name Siloam (sent) takes on double significance, memorializing the obedience of the blind man and the higher obedience of Christ as coming into the world at the Father's behest to be the light and life of men.

For the neighbors the cure was of intense personal interest. They had first of all a problem of identification, for seeing eyes can mean a veritable transformation of personality (vss. 8-9). The erstwhile beggar settled their dispute handily. He was the formerly blind man, and no mistake. After the *who* was settled, the *how* remained to be investigated. It is worthy of notice that the man did not try to capitalize on his sudden fame by making the miracle sound grandiose. It would have been so easy to manufacture a few details. He is content with the truth. That sort of a person is more useful to Christ than the one who exaggerates when he relates his personal testimony.

A hint of impending trouble is conveyed by the conjunction of two things. First, the man is conducted to the Pharisees; second, the day of the miracle was the Sabbath (vss. 13-14). These leaders could be expected to raise the issue of violation of the Sabbath rest. From the man's report they felt they had ample evidence for their complaint. The only catch was that the work was so humane and so unique. Could a sinner accomplish such a result? No wonder some of the

Pharisees shook their heads. They were really perplexed (vs. 16).

As a diversion from their own debate, the leaders interrogate the man before them. What is his opinion of his benefactor? The answer—*he is a prophet*—rests on the fact that many prophets of old performed wonders, and now that John the Baptist had appeared (though he did no miracle) the order of prophets had apparently been instituted afresh.

It might still be possible, the Pharisees reasoned, to deny the miracle altogether if the parents could be persuaded to testify that their son had not been blind (vs. 18). But the parents were not very helpful, as they admitted that their son was sightless from birth. Their unwillingness to say more was dictated by fear of the Jews. They preferred to let the son assume whatever risk attended the narration of his cure. It is not clear just how much was involved in the threat of putting confessors of Jesus as the Christ out of the synagogue (cf. 16:2). Westcott speaks of it as "exclusion from all religious fellowship."

After getting nowhere with the parents, the rulers decided on a second examination of the son (vs. 24). By charging him to *give God the praise* they were admonishing him to disclose all he knew in this matter (cf. Josh. 7:19). And then they tried to put words in his mouth—tampering with a witness by asserting that Jesus was a sinner (cf. vs. 16). Just as the parents had a *know* to contribute, balanced by a *know not* (vss. 20, 21), so with the son. His personal experience did not lead him to find Jesus a sinner. He was willing to

59

leave that issue to the theologians. But he was glad to affirm what he knew positively and unshakably. He himself, once sightless, could now see (vs. 25). Jesus had made the difference. Here was the conviction and boldness which marked the apostolic witness in Jerusalem later on, which so annoyed the authorities (Acts 4:20).

At this point the investigation began to deteriorate badly, with the rulers demanding another account of the miracle, and the man before them getting impatient at their tactics. He showed his vexation by chiding his questioners. Are they interested in the details because they plan to become Jesus' disciples? The sarcasm was biting in its severity. Weakly they voiced their loyalty to Moses (vs. 28).

To match their previously asserted knowledge about Jesus (we *know* he is a sinner), the rulers now profess ignorance about Him as to His background. He is a nobody (vs. 29). It is a surprising admission in the opinion of the witness. They are the religious leaders of his people and yet they have no insight into the identity and credentials of his benefactor. It seems self-evident to his unsophisticated mind that God would not have released the power to perform such a wonderful, unheard-of miracle to one who was a sinner. The rulers were getting the worst of the argument and they knew it. Lest they be further embarrassed, they hastily concluded the interview by dismissing the man from their presence, and in doing so stooped to stigmatizing the poor fellow as blinded all his life because of sin (cf. vs. 2). It was a cruel thrust. They then cast him out, possibly in fulfillment of the threat made earlier, though he had not confessed Jesus as the Christ (cf. vs. 22). He was soon to discover that he was not cut off from divine favor and fellowship. Another stood ready to take him in (vs. 35). Jesus sought him, found him, and revealed Himself to him as the Son of Man (Greek text). In doing so, He accepted worship (cf. 20:28). This in itself demonstrates that the title *Son of Man* indicates far more than humanity.

All that remained for Jesus was to draw the two-fold lesson from this episode. The blind man was representative of a class of people who knew their limitations and gladly turned to Him for help. But the Pharisees would not admit any need, for they were proudly self-sufficient. Actually they were blind (Matt. 23:24), especially to their own corruption of heart. They refused to welcome the Light of the world. Their sin remained.

16. The Witness of the Good Shepherd (10:1-42). A close connection in thought with the previous chapter is evident. Not only is the miracle of healing fresh in the popular mind (10:21); the erstwhile blind man, though he does not appear in person, is perfectly described in the picture drawn of the sheep who respond to the shepherd. And just as clearly etched on the canvas of thought are the Pharisees (vss. 1, 10, 12, 13), who have no concern for the sheep who are supposedly under their care. The *you* (vs. 1) seems to include those who are in view at the end of Chapter 9.

By way of analysis we note that the material is divided into two fairly equal parts. First comes the presentation of Jesus as the Shepherd (vss. 1-18); then, after a transitional section (vss. 19-21), a spirited conversation between Him and the Jewish leaders over the issue of His own person (note vs. 24).

The chapter opens with a parable (vs. 6). Yet the common word for parable does not appear here. The term used means proverb or riddle. It appears again in 16:25, 29, and denotes something which involves illustration but still needs explanation. All the details are familiar to one versed in Palestinian sheep husbandry, but the spiritual truths latent here require unfolding.

By no means are the intruders to be identified with former leaders of a godly sort. The identification applies to those who make their own rules of entrance to God's kingdom and use their influence to fleece the sheep. Nothing is made of the porter here. The shepherd and the sheep are the central concerns. Of the two, the shepherd commands more attention. In ordinary life this might not be true, for he could be very inconspicuous, just an element taken for granted. But here nothing which the sheep do is seen independently of him. He is the indispensable key to their welfare— his call leads them out to pasture and his position at the head of the flock constrains the sheep to follow him. No other can take his place (vs. 5).

The parable fell on deaf ears (vs. 6; cf. 9:41; Mark 4:11-12). Graciously the Lord drew out its implications for the benefit of His hearers. The door and the shepherd are distinct in the parable (vs. 2), but now they are both applied to Him (vss. 7, 11). This is fully justified, for the door is a figure of salvation (vs. 9) whereas the shepherd is the provider of life (vss. 10, 11). No matter how many the sheep may be, this shepherd knows them all, even as those who are his own know him (vs. 14).

Jesus is the *good* shepherd for another reason. He is utterly different from the thieves who come to plunder the flock (vss. 8, 10). All that ever came before Him, insofar as they offered life, were thieves and robbers—taking from Christ the unique glory of His Saviourhood and robbing the sheep by holding out false hopes. Only Christ can give life and this gift is given in abundance, for it is the very life of God and therefore inexhaustible.

As the good shepherd Jesus puts Himself likewise in contrast to the hireling. Whereas His own love for the sheep was enough to cause Him to die for them (vs. 11), the concern of these is so slight that they think more of their own comfort and security than of their responsibility to care for the sheep. They cannot, with Jesus, speak of *my* sheep. The church suffers from such as well as from wolves which rend the flock (Acts 20:29-30; cf. I Pet. 5:2).

The fold of Judaism yields the nucleus for the flock of the Good Shepherd, but He claims many more, claiming them before they are reclaimed from their wandering ways. They will hear His voice sounding out by means of the Gospel call, even though it will be spoken by men. Jesus knew He was sent to the lost sheep of the house of Israel, but He foresaw a worldwide ingathering, a great host united to Himself; *one flock* (not *fold*) and *one shepherd* (vs. 16; cf. one body . . . one Lord, Eph. 4:4-5).

Dear will be the purchase price for this almost numberless flock, even the life-blood of the Son of God. But it will be gladly, freely paid. His death will be as little a matter of human pressure as of divine compulsion. Though the Father will not compel this sacrifice, He will meet it with an answering and rewarding love (vs. 17). With the same freedom that lays His life on the altar, Jesus promises to take it again. He knows that death cannot hold Him (vs. 18).

These words of Jesus, culminating in the promise of His redeeming death and resurrection, were unacceptable to *many* of the Jews, who chose to revive the charge that the speaker was demon-possessed and therefore mad (Matt. 12:24). By their blindness and stubbornness they advertised the fact that they did not belong to the Lord's flock. Still *others* could not be persuaded that insanity justly described Jesus. How could such words be the product of madness? They could not forget the good work done on the blind man. Once again Jesus produced cleavage (cf. 7:43; 9:16; cf. Luke 12:51).

The last time notice placed our Lord in Jerusalem at the Feast of Tabernacles (7:2), which came in the fall of the year. Now winter has set in (10:22), and people are observing the Feast of Dedication, commemorating the recapture of Jerusalem by Jewish patriots under Judas Maccabeus in the days of the Maccabean revolt against Syria. The temple, defiled by the pagan ruler Antiochus Epiphanes, was cleansed and restored to the worship of God.

Despite the interval, the words of Jesus about the good shepherd were not forgotten. The Jews crowded around Him in the temple, pressing Him to assert Himself on the issue of Messiahship (vs. 24). The believer knows that Jesus is the Christ; He has the witness of the Spirit (I John 5:5-6), but the unbeliever has no sure ground of confidence that Jesus is *not* what He claimed to be. That is why unbelief cannot quite leave Jesus alone. His claims keep disturbing the otherwise quiet sea of religious self-satisfaction.

Our Lord's words had been plain enough. To come right out and assert that He was the Christ would not involve a higher claim than He had made (5:17; 8:12; 10:7, 11, etc.). It would only elicit anew the charge of blasphemy and inflame the adversaries. So Jesus simply points to His *works* (vs. 25). The difficulty is not with His credentials, but with the unwillingness of the nation to receive them and so receive Him. These leaders lack faith and thereby proclaim that they do not belong to His sheep (vs. 26). Judaism, of which they boasted, was not the same as the flock over which He would preside (cf. vs. 16).

One of His greatest works is the eternal provision He makes for His sheep. No power can pluck them from His protective grasp, which is coupled with the Father's (vs. 29). This is but a reaffirmation of what Jehovah is expected to do for His own as the Shepherd (Ps. 23). The two who thus collaborate are really one in essence, in purpose, and in work—Father and

Son (vs. 30). Jesus has met the challenge of the Jews (see vs. 24) by expressing His Messiahship in terms of equality with the Father. The offense cut deeply and violence threatened on the spot (vs. 31).

Are the Jews assaulting Him for a *good* work, Jesus demands to know, with a trace of sad irony? No, it is the person, not the work—the person Jesus alleges Himself to be. This is the crux of difference always. Is He one who came down from Heaven, humbling Himself to minister to men, or is He a mere man exalting Himself to the rank of deity (vs. 33)?

Jesus meets the challenge by an appeal to Scripture. In Psalm 82, God calls the judges of Israel gods (Elohim) because they are appointed to do a work which is peculiarly God's. It is His province to judge. If such a use of language is legitimate, how much more the confession of Jesus that He is the Son of God, seeing that God has both sanctified and sent Him into the world, so that He has a uniqueness that these men of old did not have (vs. 36)?

The claim of Jesus could only be substantiated before the natural man by appropriate works which approved His heavenly station, so He returns to this emphasis (vss. 37-38). But stony hearts rejected the word once again and demonstrated their unbelief by a further attempt to apprehend their prey as a dangerous enemy (vs. 39). Withdrawing to one of the haunts of John the Baptist beyond the Jordan, Jesus by this move turned back the thoughts of men to John's witness concerning Him. John himself, for all his greatness, performed no sign. He had opened no blind

66

eyes. But his testimony to the superiority of the One coming after him had been abundantly borne out. Unbelief would have to doubt John as well as Jesus to be consistent. Many were not willing to go that far (vs. 42).

17. The Witness of Lazarus' Resurrection (11:1-57). This incident, unreported in the Synoptics, finds a place in this Gospel for at least two reasons. First, it brought to a head the growing antagonism of the religious authorities toward Jesus and directly contributed to His death. Second, it is doubtless intended to portray by anticipation the victory of the Lord over death in His own case (cf. 10:18). As a miracle, this event climaxed the demonstration that the whole gamut of human need, death included, can be met by the compassion and power of the Son of God.

To readers of the Synoptic Gospels Martha and Mary are no strangers (Luke 10:38-42). But in this case, as in others, John supplements the Synoptic tradition, for he brings Lazarus to the fore, about whom Luke is silent. But John's characterization of the two sisters is thoroughly in accord with Luke's—Martha, assuming responsibility so energetically, Mary living in the deeps of a quiet, thoughtful spirit, yet both so thoroughly one in devotion to Jesus.

John is explicit as to the location of the home of these three. It was Bethany, a town about two miles east of Jerusalem. He also identifies Mary as the woman, unnamed in the Gospels, who anointed Jesus at a supper in her town (Mark 14:3).

Lazarus might never have appeared in Scripture were it not for his sickness. His own condition was appeal enough; the message of the sisters to the absent Lord contained no entreaty of their own. Human need always struck a responsive chord in Jesus. How much more when a beloved friend lay languishing!

The paradox of apparent apathy (the Saviour made no move for two days) despite love for Lazarus is solved by Jesus' comment that this sickness was for the glory of God (vs. 4). Other sicknesses have proved to be so, in different ways (II Cor. 12:7; Gal. 4:13).

Jesus, knowing what He would do, as always, found it expedient to share His intention with the disciples, for they were always with Him (vss. 7-16). First, He shocked them by announcing a return to Judea. It seemed a foolhardy plan to His companions. After all, they had come away from Judea a short time before because of violent opposition (10:39-40). The Master assured His anxious followers that He was not stumbling along uncertainly in the dark (vss. 9-10; cf. 8: 12; 9:5). The disciples can safely follow Him, even though it seems perilous.

A second purpose of this conversation with the Twelve was to explain what had happened to Lazarus and to set forth His own purpose with respect to the dead man. He put the matter cryptically (Lazarus will be awakened out of sleep) but this was not an entirely new way of speaking of death (Mark 5:35-39). It became standard in the early Church (Acts 7:60; I Thess. 4:13-14).

The disciples will profit by this experience, for it

will quicken and deepen their faith in the Lord Jesus (vs. 15). Faith is a growing experience (2:11; 13:19; 14:1; 20:8). Every opportunity to exercise it strengthens the tie with the Son of God.

Bethany was astir with life when Jesus reached it, though death reigned in its midst. Friends had gathered, some from nearby Jerusalem, to offer condolences. It was not easy for the Lord to see the sisters in private. When this was achieved, first with Martha, then with Mary, the same comment rose spontaneously to their lips (vss. 21, 32). How often in those first dreadful hours after death visited their home they had shared this common thought. Death, they knew, had never occurred in the presence of the Lord. Why, oh why, could He not have been there? It would be only natural if a tincture of bitterness mingled with regret here, but there is no open blame for the delay in coming.

It is exceedingly difficult to get a clear picture of Martha's expectation. She has confidence that God will grant anything Jesus asks (vs. 22). This would logically include resurrection, for she must have known that the Saviour had raised people from the dead. Yet, when Jesus promises resurrection for Lazarus, she does not seize upon it as a present reality, but interprets it in terms of resurrection at the last day (vs. 24). At the tomb she shows no expectation of the miracle that will banish her sorrow (vs. 39).

Jesus does His best to energize and lift the level of her faith without telling her in so many words what He proposes to do. He points to Himself (vs. 25). Because He is *the life,* He must also be *the resurrection.*

If death can successfully resist Him, He is not life in the ultimate and absolute sense. All that He is for the future (resurrection at the last day) He is now. What will be openly, sweepingly done then can be done now for His friend Lazarus. Believers in Jesus have tasted of the powers of the coming age. There is no qualitative difference between Jesus' power in the days of His flesh and that power exhibited in the last days.

The dead in Christ have promise of resurrection (vs. 25) and the living saints shall never die, that is, never be brought under the reign of death which Christ will break by His own resurrection (vs. 26; cf. Rom. 6:9).

Martha, like Simon Peter, could affirm faith in Jesus' person even though her understanding of His work was clouded (vs. 27; cf. Matt. 16:16, 22). Her confession coincides with that of the followers of Jesus as a whole (John 20:31; Acts 9:20, 22).

This conversation took place outside the town (vs. 30). There Jesus remained till Mary came to the spot and fell at His feet to weep out her sorrow (vs. 32). Moved by the sight of His dear friend, followed as she was by mourners who could do nothing but show their sympathy by their presence, Jesus felt he could wait no longer to act. It was time to proceed toward the tomb (vs. 34). Even so, His own tears had begun to fall. Faced with an accumulation of pain and anguish and sorrow for three years such as others do not meet in a lifetime, Jesus never allowed His contact with suffering to harden Him or make Him impatient with human weakness. His second groaning (vs. 38) was due to the fact that the mourners interpreted His tears as a token of impotence. He seemed as powerless as they in the face of death (vss. 37-38). But it was no time for argument. It was the hour for deeds. *Take ye away the stone!*

Family pride was piqued by this command. It was time for plain speaking. Martha intervened to remark that decay had already set in. The opening of the sepulcher would only bring an unpleasant experience to add to the pain which death had already inflicted. Again the dark side of providence flashes momentarily, as it did when sickness claimed its victim a few days before. The Lord permits the momentary suffering that His friends may be surprised by joy. In such an hour, how daring are the words *believe . . . see* the glory of God (vs. 40). Here God's glory is His power to reverse corruption. No wonder the resurrection bodies of the saints are called bodies of glory (I Cor. 15:43).

Before speaking to the deceased, Jesus speaks to the Father, and His prayer is simply a word of thanks. So complete is the accord between the Son and the Father that a miscarriage of prayer is unthinkable. What the people hear confesses that accord. What they are about to see exhibits it. *Lazarus, come forth.* The name restricts the movement within the realm of the dead. In the coming day all will hear and respond (5:28).

The friends are permitted to free the resurrected Lazarus from his bandages (funeral wrappings). They can do this, whereas only one could loose the bonds of death (vs. 44). Just here the writer could so easily have injected a few words describing the glad reunion

71

of brother and sisters, but he passes over it. This is a Gospel. More important by far is the sketching of the effect of the miracle in terms of faith and unbelief (vss. 45-46).

News of the great sign was soon the topic of conversation in the highest circles of Jerusalem and it contributed directly to a fresh and determined effort to put Jesus to death (vss. 47-54). The Pharisees in the council were believers in the resurrection as a theological dogma, whereas the chief priests, being Sadducees, were not (cf. Acts 23:6-10). But this issue did not suffice to divide them here, for they felt obliged to combine forces in order to combat the influence of Jesus, lest this latest demonstration of His power bring on a popular revolutionary movement which Rome would act to crush. In the process the Jews' *place* (temple?) and very existence as a privileged *nation* would be menaced (vs. 48). The mood of frustration was broken by the cold-blooded dynamism of the high priest Caiaphas. They did not know how to handle the situation, but he did. It was a simple solution which he propounded—get rid of the troublemaker and the trouble will cease (vs. 50). To John it was noteworthy that the high priest's counsel should be phrased in language which, though intended to be merely the formulation of a course of expediency, was nevertheless framed in terms of substitutionary atonement. God makes even the wrath of men to praise him (Ps. 76:10). In commenting on the unconscious prophecy of Caiaphas, John notes that the death of Christ actually embraced not the one nation only but the children of God scattered everywhere. It is assumed that the acceptance of the death of Messiah will be needed in order to make them God's children (cf. 1:12).

The agreement of the council on a plan of action necessitated Jesus' withdrawal, for His time had not yet fully come (vs. 54; cf. 4:1-3). The remainder of the chapter is transitional, reflecting both the strength of popular interest in Jesus and the determination of the authorities to put him to death (vss. 55-57).

18. The Witness of Mary of Bethany (12:1-11). On the eve of the beginning of holy week, Jesus' friends whom He had just blessed so richly sought to honor Him with a feast. Though Lazarus was there as a participant, beyond question Jesus was the honored guest. The parts played by the two sisters are in strict accord with what is revealed elsewhere—Martha attending to the physical needs, Mary concerned with spiritual things. Her grief is now put away. Joy and gratitude rule her spirit as she pours a thank-offering of ointment upon the Lord's feet and proceeds to wipe them with her tresses. No doubt the fragrance of the ointment testified to its high quality.

Judas, his tongue suddenly loosed by the wave of disappointment which engulfed him at the sight of this "waste," protested strenuously. It mattered not that a grateful woman's spirit was crushed by his thoughtless outburst or that the Master was depreciated, as though unworthy of so lavish a gift. All that mattered was that the equivalent of a tidy sum of money was vanishing before the greedy eyes of the betrayer. His professed concern for the poor was only a smoke screen. This rascal had been stealing from the common purse over which he had charge (vs. 6).

Jesus wasted little time on Judas. One curt word put him in his place. A testimony to Mary is wrapped up in the same sentence—"Let her alone, that she may keep it for the day of my burial." It is not clear how Mary could keep what she had just freely poured out. We must suppose that the Lord is commending her for anointing His body so near the time for burial. The lesson is plain. Jesus appreciates a ministry to His own person. The poor are never impoverished by that which is bestowed upon the Son of God. They are made the richer in Him who is their proven friend and helper.

Bethany had been put on the map by the miracle of recent days. Throngs of curious people continued to flow out of Jerusalem to see the two principals (vs. 9). The rulers, moved with envy (cf. Mark 15:10), seriously considered including Lazarus in their plans for murder, simply because he was a living testimony to Jesus (we have no recorded word from his lips). These Jews who *went away* to Jesus were defecting from the hold which the rulers had exercised. This, rather than a physical movement, must be understood here (vs. 11).

19. The Witness of Palm Sunday (12:12-19). Pilgrims had already begun to pour into the city for the *feast* of Passover. Word was passed from one to another that Jesus was leaving Bethany for Jerusalem,

74

so that crowds in a festive mood surged out of the city to join the smaller company that left Bethany with Him. That this was a special occasion was attested by the circumstance that Jesus had secured a mount, thus fulfilling the prophecy of Zechariah 9:9 (vs. 15).

One of the prime motifs of this Gospel is the setting forth of the wide divergence between the people and Jesus in the understanding of His mission. As in John 6, the people are bent on having Him as their king in an ordinary earthly sense. This is indicated in several ways: by the title *King of Israel;* by *Hosanna* ("save now"); by the waving of *palm* branches, a recognized symbol of Jewish independence since the early days of the Maccabees; and by the fact that the raising of Lazarus (vs. 18) excited the throng with its demonstration of power. That power could be used to break the hold of the living (Rome) as well as to conquer death.

Meanwhile the Pharisees, previously despondent over Jesus' popularity, but given leadership by the Sadducee Caiaphas (11:49-50) and hope that they could rid themselves of this trouble-maker, are plunged again into despair by the wave of enthusiasm which has swept Jesus triumphantly into the stronghold of the opposition. It looks now as though Caiaphas' plan cannot be carried through. Popular sentiment in Jesus' favor is too strong (vs. 19).

20. The Witness of Jesus in the Shadow of the Cross (12:20-50). From the words which follow, revealing our Lord's understanding of His mission, it becomes apparent that both groups are wrong. To be

sure, He is Israel's king, but He is not offering a kingdom such as the Son of David was expected to inaugurate. As the ancient prophecy (see vs. 15) had stated, He was a meek king, one having salvation. This was not the day of His power but of His passion. By the same token the Pharisees were wrong, for they would be able to accomplish their will against Jesus after all, but not because He deserved to die. Rather, because it was designed that He should die and so fulfill the divine purpose.

The occasion for this disclosure of the Lord's thoughts was the effort of certain *Greeks* to gain an interview with Him (vss. 20-21). Already attracted to Judaism, as were many other Gentiles, they had come to Jerusalem to worship the God of the Jews (cf. Acts 8:27). A figure of Jesus' stature held great interest for them.

Their desire for an interview, however, remained unfulfilled. What follows is directed to the disciples and others who stood by. The gist of it is that to *see Jesus* is of little value unless one sees Him in death (vss. 24, 32). That message will be taken to the Greeks, and if they receive it they will have eternal life. Again, as in John 6, the popular expectation of Messiahship as a king of worldly features is set aside for a Messiahship which finds its fulfillment in death.

Two descriptions of this death follow (vss. 24, 32). One involves going down into the earth, and has a kind of analogue in the burial of Jesus, though the specific figure is of seed—planting and harvest (vs. 24). Death spells a reproduced life—*much fruit.* Christ as teacher and miracle-worker does not save by these activities. Salvation turns on His death. One must know Him as the Crucified. The same conception—a life laid down —is central to the law of discipleship (vs. 25). The servant is not greater than his Lord. Apparent loss brings eternal gain.

Before going on to the second description of His death, Jesus gives expression to His own natural, human shrinking from this ordeal. It is John's equivalent of the Gethsemane agony (vs. 27; cf. Matthew 26:38). There is the same appeal to the Father for help and the same realization that the experience set before Him is inescapable if He would fulfill His mission. Likewise there is a recognition of Satanic pressure as the Cross is faced (vs. 31) and a confidence in His victory over the powers of darkness.

At length Jesus comes to the second portrayal of His death. Here the description is not that of going down, but of being lifted up (vs. 32; cf. 3:14). The emphasis is the same, however, as with the grain of wheat; the results of that death are staggering in their outreach. The Greeks are representative of a vast company—*all men*—who will come under the drawing power of the Cross (cf. 6:44). No wonder the Lord could see in His death a true glorification (vs. 23).

But the people who heard Him were puzzled, for they could not understand how the Son of Man could die. If Jesus was equating this expression with Messiah (vs. 34; cf. vs. 23), His Christology was confusing. His hearers thought of the Messiah as king, and they had learned to look for the Son of Man as a heavenly figure who would suddenly appear to judge and rule (Daniel 7:13-14; also the Book of Enoch). Hence the puzzled question, Who is *this* Son of Man? Jesus stood alone in perceiving that His mission called for death.

One cannot help feeling the tragedy in the closing words to the people (vss. 35-36). It is a last appeal to *believe in* the light (cf. 1:7-9) and to walk in it. The nation, like its leaders, was refusing its God who had revealed Himself in His Son. Henceforth the Lord Jesus would be devoting Himself to His own (chaps. 13-17). The parallel with Matthew 23:37-39 is striking.

It only remains for John to set forth the depth of that darkness and the tenacity of that unbelief (vss. 37-43) before picturing in one brief scene the final summary of the rejected Christ (vss. 44-50).

Israel's unbelief flourished despite *miracles—so many* of them. It flourished despite prophecy, which might have been taken as a warning (Isaiah 53:1 ff.). Another word from Isaiah (6:9-10) had pre-written this judgment. It was not arbitrary, but rather a judicial hardening. Opportunity long neglected evokes no response. The conscience seared by repeated violation ceases to function. Thus the nation, steeled to resist the claims of Jesus, *could not believe.* What appears at first sight to be a welcome exception to the general rule only proves in the end to make the rule more dismally binding and complete. What movement to faith existed among *many* of the *chief rulers* was abortive. It did not rise to the point of willingness to confess

78

Jesus. Fear of men was more powerful than the desire to honor God (vs. 43). This is pseudo-faith (cf. 2: 23-25; 8:30 ff.).

The closing testimony of Jesus reiterates the familiar themes of His ministry: His faithful representation of the Father (vss. 44-45), the need for faith in Himself (vs. 46), the peril of rejecting Him (vs. 48), the blessing of everlasting life for those who respond (vs. 50).

III. The Witness of the Son of God to His Own (13:1—17:26)

Having spoken His last words to the nation (12:44-50), it remained for Jesus to share His parting thoughts with His disciples (13-16) and to pray for them (17). The setting, as it appears in the other Gospels, was the Upper Room, where the Lord had gone to eat the Passover with his own. John's account says nothing about the institution of the Lord's Supper, but dwells on the teaching ministry of Christ during the evening hours.

1. The foot washing (13:1-17). Jesus' *hour,* so often referred to, is now about to strike. It brings re-union with the Father, but also separation from His chosen band. Shepherd and sheep are about to be parted. This adds poignancy to every act and word, for everything is bathed in a love that now reaches its zenith (*end* in verse 1 means uttermost in quality). John 10:11 is the best commentary.

Supper being ended (vs. 2) is not the reading of the best manuscripts, which have "while supper was in progress." Satan, able to penetrate even this holy place through his control of Judas, appears in sharp contrast to Jesus. He has purposed that Judas, who has long been playing into his hands, should betray Jesus. Hate burned that night as well as love.

What Jesus is about to do in the foot washing is presented in the light of His own understanding of His dignity and worth. God has sent Him. God was receiving Him back. All authority was His (vs. 3). Yet he was willing to stoop to perform this lowly task. And He proposed to do it aright, not in some condescending token fashion, but stripped for action as a servant would be, doing the work Himself with basin and towel. The disciples were His servants and should have performed this service for Him (vs. 16). Instead, He was doing it for them. He was doing it, furthermore, in the spirit of self-humbling which brought Him from God to bathe the world in His redeeming love and grace.

Possibly Peter was the first to receive this ministration and he protested the unfitness of it. He did not *know* what it was intended to impart (note the contrast with Jesus' knowledge in vs. 3). When informed that the act had more than external meaning, he was ready to have his other extremities included as well (vs. 9). In replying, Jesus indicated that Peter had already been washed (*louō,* the complete body bath, Titus 3:5), something which was not true of Judas the unregenerate (vs. 11). Peter still had need for the washing (*niptō,* used of the washing of individual members of the body) of his feet. Sin comes to the believer in the course of his walk in this sinful world. The one cleansing is unrepeatable, the other occurs as needed (I John 1:9).

Jesus' ministration had still another meaning (vss. 13-17). It spoke by way of example concerning a life of humble service by one disciple toward another (vs. 14). One senses here a parallel to "as I have loved you, that ye also love one another" (vs. 34). In fact, if love is not present, the outward act of service means nothing (I Cor. 13:3). What is in view ultimately is not a ceremony of foot washing which loses its reality where people wear shoes and walk on pavement, but a voluntary outpouring of dedicated ministry to the saints, taking whatever form is needed.

2. The Separation of Judas (13:18-30). Once again the Saviour makes a distinction between the Eleven and Judas (vs. 18; cf. vss. 10, 11). He does not deny that He chose him to discipleship. In fact, only as the act of a disciple could the pathos of Judas' betrayal be felt, as the Scripture had indicated. Just as Jesus' nation rejected him (1:11) His own disciple will betray Him. The Lord has lived with this awful prospect. Now He speaks of it, that in coming days the faithful ones may recognize that their leader was not "taken in" by a false follower. Rather, nothing was hidden from His understanding.

Yet Jesus could not take this defection lightly. His spirit was troubled by it (vs. 21). As long as Judas was present as a reminder of treachery, the fellowship between the Lord and his own could not be unhindered. The public announcement of the betrayal brought consternation to the little company, but it served its purpose by leading to anxious questioning which resulted in the elimination of Judas from the midst. Only John was permitted to know the identity of the betrayer (vss.

25-26), and not by name. John was given to know that the Saviour's heart, when fairly breaking with sorrow, was still capable of compassionate love. The identification of the betrayer would come through extending to him the choice morsel from the meal as a gesture of kindness. Judas was being treated as the honored guest (vs. 26). Ironically, with the sop not Jesus but Satan entered Judas to goad him to betrayal and then to self-destruction. To receive from Jesus is something vastly different from receiving *Him.*

A quiet word, quickly spoken in low voice from the Master to the now demonized disciple, secured his departure. It created no stir because the rest assumed that he was going on a mission connected with his duties as treasurer. Judas went out, his 'soul enveloped in the blackness of sin's gloom and despair. Gehenna was already opening its cavernous mouth to receive him (vs. 30).

3. The Departing Lord and His Abiding Commandment (13:31-35). Turning from the dark side of the ordeal before him, Jesus now sees it in the light of His appointed mission. As in 12:23, our Lord sees Himself glorified at the Cross, and the Father likewise. Beyond the Cross lies reunion with the Father. This spells separation from the disciples, who must remain, but their spirits are not to be filled with sadness. To be His disciples in truth they must have *love* one for the other, that quality of love already felt in Christ and so soon to be poured out at the Cross. If love is present, the absent Lord will not be absent after all, but still living and speaking to *all* men as His love grips and governs his own (vs. 35).

4. The Prophecy Regarding Peter (13:36-38). Simon was too concerned with Jesus' words about departure to think seriously about love's imperative, though he would do so in time (cf. I Peter 1:22). He was inquisitively curious about Jesus' plans, and a bit resentful that he was not included. As one of the earliest followers of the Galilean, and the acknowledged leader of them, he was ready to vindicate Jesus' choice. Perhaps this would bring comfort and compensation in the light of the impending betrayal. Little did he know his own weakness under pressure. Our Lord warns him against any impetuous display of devotion. It can only issue in repeated denial (cf. Luke 22:31-34). The double announcement of betrayal and denial came as a terrible shock to the disciples. Jesus read it on their faces and began to spell out His message of comfort and cheer.

5. The Coming Reunion (14:1-6). Between the announcement of the Lord's departure and the intimation of defection and weakness in their own ranks, the disciples were distraught beyond measure. Hearts were troubled and agitated. But every occasion for distress is a fresh call to confidence in God and in His Son. Both *believe* clauses are probably imperative in their force. Faith must now span the chasm between the seen and the unseen, and to do so must build upon all that Jesus had demonstrated to His own of Himself and the Father (cf. 3:12). The parting would not be permanent. From the house in Jerusalem the gaze of the disciples is directed to another in glory—*the Father's house.* Whereas they must go forth from these borrowed quarters to face the uncertainties of the night, they can look on to a provision that is eternal. *Mansions* await them, that is, abiding places. There will be no more departures, no more heart-rending farewells. Just as two of their number had preceded them into this Jerusalem chamber to get it ready for the feast, so the Lord was going ahead to *prepare* the home above for the coming of His own (vs. 2). And all this would be done with a view to gathering them about Him for the eternal reunion. Heaven would be merely a change of locale if Jesus were absent, but with Him in the midst it will be the acme of bliss.

The *way* by which Jesus reaches the Father ought to be clear to these men (vs. 4), for He had over and over emphasized that He must die and rise again. Thomas professes ignorance both of the destination and the road by which Jesus will reach it (vs. 5). The Lord who gives the answer is Himself the answer. He is the indispensable *way* to the Father, for He alone is able to reveal in Himself the full *truth* about God (cf. 1:14-18), and more than that, He provides the *life* of God to all who come to God by Him. Life is the word which predominates in the "I am's" of our Lord.

6. **The Privilege of Knowing the Father through the Son** (14:7-14). Thomas' question had revealed ignorance of Jesus as the way to the Father. Philip's

outburst laid bare a more serious ignorance. By confessing his desire to see the Father, he admitted his failure to understand that the Father stood revealed in the Son. Repeatedly the Lord had stated this great truth in His public teaching (8:19; 10:30, 38). It was out of this union between Father and Son that the *words* of Jesus had come (cf. 8:28; 12:49) and the *works* as well (cf. 5:36; 10:25, 32, 37). If the words were too lofty for human comprehension, then the works should be allowed their convincing witness (vs. 11). Almost imperceptibly the Lord has dropped the word *know* and put in its place the word *believe.* One can only know spiritual truth by approaching through the door of faith (cf. II Tim. 1:12). And so it is with works also. They will issue from faith in the Son (vs. 12). Jesus had promised *greater works* to the people in the wake of one of His notable signs (5:20). Here He promises them to His disciples, not to be done for them but through them. But since such works—greater in number but not in quality—will come to pass because Jesus is going to the Father, they will really be accomplished by the risen Lord (cf. Romans 15:18-19). They cannot be expected automatically, but in answer to prayer (vss. 13-14). No limit is put upon the ministry of prayer as long as requests are made in Jesus' name. This involves recognition that the disciple can contribute nothing but his expectation, grounded in faith, that the risen Lord will work mightily as of old. In this, too, the Father and the Son are inseparable, for the Father is glorified in the Son.

7. Obedience and the Gift of the Spirit (14:15-21). Though the Lord will be absent, His commandments will linger as the expression of His will. Love for Him will linger also and serve as the inspiration for keeping the commandments (vs. 15). This obedience will pave the way for the coming of the Spirit as Christ's gift. Though the Spirit is sovereignly bestowed, His effective operation depends on the obedience of the saints (Acts 5:32). Strikingly, Jesus states the gift of the Spirit as the result of His own prayer to the Father. If the Son must pray in this fashion, what a light this casts on the need of the disciples to pray.

Certain important disclosures are made here about the Spirit. He is called a Paraclete. This is rendered *Comforter* in our common version, but this is misleading unless we revert to the Latin derivation of this word and so arrive at the meaning *Strengthener.* The Lord Jesus had been an unfailing source of inspiration and strength to His followers. Now *another* was coming in His place. This implies no inferiority, hence no loss to the disciples through the exchange (cf. 16:7). Actually the Lord is not leaving them except in a physical sense, as the sequel in our present passage makes clear. But the immediate emphasis is upon the abiding presence of the Spirit—*for ever* (vs. 16).

In what ways will the Spirit prove to be a Strengthener? Two areas are specified. First, He will strengthen by His instruction and counsel. In this capacity He is called *the Spirit of truth* (vs. 17; cf. 15:26; 16:13). Christ, as the truth (14:6), has been the teacher of these men. Now this other Counselor would take up this task. A second sphere of His strengthening activity, closely related to His teaching, is disclosed in 15: 26-27. Despite pressure and hostility from the world, the disciples will be able to bear a witness to their Lord because of the Spirit's witness in and through them.

The world is unable to receive the Spirit (cf. I Cor. 2:14), being unable to see Him (I Cor. 2:9) or know Him (I Cor. 2:11). Yet believers know Him as an abiding, inner presence (vs. 17). As Christ is a divider of men, so is the Spirit who comes in His name.

The Spirit will indeed be a solace to these wounded and lonely hearts. But the Lord Himself will come to minister to them, lest they be "orphans" (vs. 18). This is not His return, as in verse 3, but His contact with them through His resurrection appearances, as the next verse demonstrates. The world saw Christ no more after His ordeal at Calvary, but He appeared to His own and made them partakers of His risen life. What this means is stated in surpassingly wonderful terms— not only that their Lord belongs to the glory, one with the Father, but that they have the focal point of their spiritual life in Christ and that He indwells them (vs. 20). This is life indeed! Mortal men, sinful men, caught up into the life of God!

Lest this life be thought of as mere existence, Jesus defines it in terms of *love*. Love for the Master brings a share in the Father's love and that of the Son, for the two are one in love as in all else. As long as love for Christ reigns in the heart, it will bring repeated manifestations of the Lord, even though the post-resurrection meetings have come to an end and the Saviour has gone into Heaven (vs. 21).

8. Special Provisions Made by the Departing Lord (14:22-31). The first of these is His own unfailing, continuing presence, shared by the Father (vs. 23). Jesus had promised to manifest Himself (vs. 21), but the constant indwelling was still more precious. *Abode* is identical with the word rendered *mansion* in verse 2. The heavenly abiding places were alluring enough, but they were remote. Here time and space are obliterated. Christ promises to dwell with His people.

A second provision concerns the Spirit. He had been mentioned by the Lord as the great gift for the days ahead (vss. 16-17), but now one of His principal offices is disclosed. He will be the teacher. Jesus had been such in a superlative sense. Quite naturally the Spirit will not ignore this groundwork, but will recall it so as to build upon it (vs. 26).

Peace is still another provision, and this peace bears Christ's own stamp. It is His in a special way. The world cannot bestow such a gift, for it does not possess it. There is no peace to the wicked. When the peace of Christ reigns, the heart is untroubled and unafraid (vs. 27). That peace faces an immediate test, for the Saviour is about to leave them. But since He is going to the Father, they who remain should *rejoice* rather than lament. True, *the prince of this world* stands in the path. He will seek to set a wedge between Father and Son. But he will fail. He cannot gain a foothold on this holy ground. He faces One who is prepared to

89

comply with the Father's *commandment,* cost what it will (vs. 31).

9. The abiding life (15:1-11). Union with Christ, already proclaimed in 14:20, is given a special turn here, one which assures a blessed and continuing relation with the Lord, even though He is taken from His own. As the *true vine,* the vine of highest spiritual potency, Christ has a position which relates Him both to God the Father and to His followers. As the *husbandman* (literally, worker of the ground—a lowly title for God Almighty, indeed) the Father directs everything. It is for His sake that the fruit is produced (cf. vs. 8).

Each believer in Jesus is a *branch* in the vine. He is considered here only from the standpoint of producing *fruit* (vs. 2). If for some reason he fails in this, He may expect the Father to remove him. It is a dubious interpretation which gives to *taketh away* the force of "lifts up" (from an unhealthy state). Out of nearly a score of occurrences of this word in John, only two instances can be so understood. Removal does not connote loss of salvation. The only issue is fruit. If a gardener cannot get results, he is justified in cutting away an unproductive growth. An unfruitful Christian is a contradiction, the more so since God provides the vibrant life necessary for fruit-bearing. All that is required of the child of God is readiness to be a channel of the divine life.

To insure maximum yield, the Father deals with the fruit-bearing branches also, removing any hindering thing so that the objective of *more fruit* may be attained (vs. 2). This process is designed to maintain the *clean* status given through the communication of the message of Christ (cf. 6:63; 13:10). On the human side this process demands abiding in Christ, which is more than being in Christ as a matter of spiritual position. It is the deliberate cultivation of the bond established with Christ, by obedience and love, so that the Christ-life (*I in you*) may be experienced as a conscious reality. The condition for spiritual usefulness is identical with the natural (vs. 4). Abiding in Christ —dwelling in His fellowship and being submissive to His will—yields *much fruit*. The alternative, trying to produce fruit apart from this relationship, yields nothing but failure (vs. 5). In the natural a branch is either a fruit-producing instrument or fuel for the fire. The spiritual analogy is rewarding usefulness or the conflagration of profitless works (vs. 6; cf. I Cor. 3:12-15).

Abiding cannot be maintained apart from giving the *words* of Christ a regnant position in the heart (cf. Col. 3:16). He is honored when His word is honored (contrast 8:37). And He honors His word when the saints come pleading its promises in prayer. The "whosoever will" of salvation has its counterpart in the "what ye will" of prayer (vs. 7). We must not overlook the opportunity of bearing fruit through the prayer life. When believers are fruit-bearing, they prove themselves disciples of Christ. The assumption here is, though unexpressed, that Christ Himself bears fruit whereby the Father is glorified. This relationship is reproduced in Christ's own (vs. 8). As fruit-bearing means a movement from man God-ward through Christ, love is a movement manward from the Father through Christ. (vs. 9). But believers must *continue* (it is our word "abide" again) in this love to know its blessing and power (cf. Jude 21). Lest this sound vague and dreamy, Jesus gives it concrete definition. The divine love is activated for the Christian by keeping Christ's *commandments*. Recall that these commands include loving one another. What is more blessed than abiding in the divine love, and what is harder than keeping God's commandments? Yet they belong together, as Jesus confessed even for Himself (vs. 10). Gethsemane and Calvary were drenched with the love of God just because they were embraced as a part of the will of God. Perfect obedience—perfect realization of love—fullness of joy; such is the order for Lord and disciple alike (vs. 11).

10. **The command to love one another (15:12-17).** This section begins and ends on the same note. Christ had spoken of commandments (vs. 10), but here He names only one, for it includes all others (Matthew 22:36-40). Yet loving the brethren seems an impossible assignment when it is bracketed with Christ's love for us. How can we love as He loves? The only satisfying answer is found in the truth that the love of Christ becomes our love which flows out to other believers. It is given to us for just this purpose.

The measure of Christ's love is His readiness to die for these men who are His *friends*. As He expresses this love for them in death, they can surely express it toward one another in life. If they are not prepared to do this, they cannot rightly be called His friends (vs. 14). As proof that He has made these obscure men His friends, Jesus offers the incontestable fact that He has not dealt with them as servants but has admitted them to the very counsels of God, withholding nothing. One does not do this with servants (vs. 15). Yet the friendship is not that of equals who contribute alike to the relationship. Christ has taken the initiative by choosing them and setting them apart to be useful (a servant may work and yet not necessarily be fruitful; as friends they cannot fail). He has already taught them that they must abide to have fruit. Here He promises that their fruit will abide (*remain* is the same word). Since they are to *go* in order to bear fruit, redeemed lives are the fruit, those who partake of eternal life (vs. 16). Fruitbearing comes through prayer as well as testimony (cf. vs. 7).

11. **Prediction of opposition from the world (15: 18—16:4).** Not every contact with unsaved men will be fruitful unto life eternal. Insofar as men partake of the spirit of *the world*—sinful humanity under the sway of Satan—they will show their hatred for the emissaries of the Cross. How imperative, then, that the brethren love one another. This will help them to bear up against the foe.

The world's attitude must not be reckoned strange. It is completely natural in the sense that the world loves its own kind, but detests the other-worldliness of the Lord's people. It neither understands it nor appreciates it. Rather, it bitterly resents it (vs. 19). Again, the world's treatment of the Lord Jesus, spelled out in an intensity of hatred that brought persecution, finds an extension in the treatment meted out to His followers (vs. 20). Ultimately this is proof that the world is estranged from God (vs. 21).

By His coming and penetrating preaching against sin, Jesus had stirred up a hornet's nest. No longer could men pass as holy or even respectable. They had no covering for their sin, and they hated the One who had exposed them. Though they might not admit it (for the Jews were proud to confess their faith in God), they were nevertheless guilty of hating God by hating the Son whom He had sent (vss. 23-24). Christ claims for Himself a passage from Psalm 69:4—they hated me *without a cause.* Such hatred is senseless, devilish, a paramount proof of human sin. Man's inhumanity to man is an old story. But man's inhumanity to the man Christ Jesus has even less excuse. It leaves him utterly condemned.

The disciples, who have been with Christ *from the beginning* and have learned of Him, must continue to bear a faithful witness to the world such as the Lord Himself had borne. They must not alter nor soften the testimony. To aid them in this, *the Spirit of truth* will be with them. He will keep them from toning down the message. He will encourage their hearts in the midst of opposition (vss. 26, 27).

Their witness will land them in difficulties. Hounded from the synagogues, they will be marked for death

(16:2). There is striking agreement between the prophecy of Jesus and the testimony of Saul the persecutor (Acts 26:9-11). It will be some consolation, when trouble strikes, to be able to recall that Jesus said it would come. They will have His sympathy and support as well as the knowledge that they are following in His steps (vs. 4). As the hour for Jesus' death approached, it was the more appropriate that He warn His followers of the solemn responsibility they had taken on themselves in bearing the cross.

12. The Coming of the Spirit (16:5-16).

Even the sobering prospect of suffering for Christ's sake did not bring heaviness of heart comparable to the loss occasioned by Jesus' departure. Christ sought to wean them from undue preoccupation with themselves to an all-absorbing sense of the greatness of His mission in which they were helpers. He was going to the Father. Let them not regard this as flight from the scene of battle and conquest. The mission had just begun. A new phase was about to open, marked by the advent of the Spirit.

What could highlight the importance of the Spirit's coming more than Jesus' assertion that it would mean advantage to the disciples over and above His own presence (vs. 7)? Our Lord adds His pledge that the Spirit will not work independently of these men any more than of the ascended Christ. His coming to the disciples will precede His coming to the world with a convicting ministry (vss. 7, 8). So it proved at Pentecost.

Sin is man's central problem. Even as Christ came to deal with it objectively at the Cross (Rom. 8:3), so the Spirit is promised to press home to sinful hearts the reality of sin and the awfulness of adding to all other offenses this crowning one of refusing the Saviour (vs. 9). The Spirit's testimony bears on the resurrection and exaltation of Christ also, for hereby the Crucified was vindicated in His claims, including the efficacy of His death (vs. 10; cf. I Tim. 3:16). Finally, the Spirit convicts of *judgment,* the one thing that is left for men if they reject the death and resurrection of the Redeemer (vs. 11). If the prince of this world is already judged and defeated by the Saviour who resisted his temptations and invaded his kingdom and broke his power at the Cross (cf. Col. 2:15), how can the worldling hope to survive the judgment?

But Jesus would magnify above all the teaching ministry which the Spirit will exercise toward believers. He will act as guide into the exciting realm of divine *truth.* Just as Jesus was content to echo the Father's words, so will this other Comforter (vs. 13). *All truth* is indeed comprehensive, for it includes *things to come* (cf. Rev. 1:10).

Lest it be thought that the Spirit, by the very importance of His ministry, will dim the luster of the Saviour and compete with Him, Jesus insists that on the contrary He Himself will be glorified by the Spirit's mission (vs. 14). The Father's resources of wisdom and power have been shared with the Son (cf. Matt. 11: 27) and now all this will be at the disposal of the Spirit to impart to Jesus' followers. Revelation, instead of diminishing, will be cumulative. Some things have not been declared by the Lord. These the Spirit will reveal (cf. vs. 12).

13. The Problem of the "little while" (16:16-24). It is a twofold interval, the first extending to Jesus' burial, the second from the entombment to the resurrection (vs. 16). The last clause of the verse is not supported by the leading manuscripts, though the words are genuine in the following verse (cf. 16:5; 14:12). Jesus did not explain the "little while" directly, but indicated that the former period would differ sharply from the latter, since the *sorrow* induced by the Lord's death and burial would be supplanted by *joy* at His reappearance. This joy will be permanent (vs. 22; cf. the *full* joy of 15:11).

The effect of the second "little while" will far outlast its brief span, for the assurance and joy engendered by seeing the risen Lord will permeate all the days which lie ahead. In the glad reunion time, questions will be put aside (vs. 23), at least of the sort which now perplex the minds of the disciples. How much the resurrection settles!

But asking in the sense of petitioning the Father in prayer will continue to be legitimate. Jesus encourages and commands it. Answered prayer will serve to perpetuate the *joy* which the resurrection brings (vs. 24).

14. The Revelation of the Father and the Overcoming of the World (16:25-33). Throughout His ministry Jesus had sought to show and interpret the

Father through His words and deeds and character. The effort had not been wholly successful (see 14:8-9). *Proverbs* (enigmatical sayings) were necessary, but revelation could soon be more *plainly* given. Surely this presupposes the teaching ministry of the Spirit, which is merely an extension of Christ's (vs. 25).

The Father will stand disclosed to these simple men as a God of love, who will lavish His affection upon them as surely as their hearts have responded to His Son (vs. 27). They must understand that it was the Son's love for the Father which took Him from glory to earth and now draws Him back to Heaven (vs. 28). The Father's love for the Son is at once the inspiration for Jesus' sacrifice on earth and also its sufficient reward.

The majesty of Jesus' words (vs. 28) is such as to lead the disciples to think they have now penetrated the mystery of the Christ-event. They are ready to attribute all knowledge to the Son and confess their faith that He has come forth from God (vs. 30). But if they do believe, their conduct in the impending crisis will not indicate it. The world—the power of its hatred for Jesus and its ability to implement its hate—will soon prove too much for this little band. These who so confidently confess their faith will be ingloriously *scattered,* leaving Jesus *alone.* Yet to Him the reality of the world will not blot out the consciousness of the Father, whose presence will not fail even though He must permit His Son to fall into the hands of sinners. This is the Saviour's consolation. The disciples may have theirs also—the knowledge that the world, so crushingly powerful as to claim the life of the mighty Son of God, stands defeated in the midst of its apparent victory. Let not those who serve the Lord Christ, therefore, be in fear of the *tribulation* which the world inflicts. It can do no more harm to them than the Cross to the triumphant Christ (vs. 33).

15. The Prayer of Christ (17:1-26). One ought not to divorce this prayer from the preceding lines. Because Jesus has overcome the world, His petitions breathe confidence as He speaks to the Father of His finished work.. And because the disciples must face tribulation in this very world which He is leaving, they are much in need of His intercessions.

Though this prayer, unlike the one found in Matthew 6:9-13, was not spoken deliberately for the purpose of giving instruction in this spiritual exercise, it nevertheless was a witness to the disciples, a revelation of the mind of Christ, fully as much as the formal teaching of the Upper Room. The disciples could the better understand their task as they perceived what things laid hold of the Master as He lifted His heart to the heavenly Father.

During His earthly ministry Jesus had claimed a unique intimacy with the Father (Matthew 11:27). This prayer corroborates His testimony. God is not someone afar off whose attention must be won by frantic appeal. He is addressed as naturally as a bosom friend who is at one's side. The Father-Son relationship comes readily to expression (vs. 1).

Insofar as the prayer bears on the work of the Son,

it finds its occasion in the arrival of the *hour.* We will probably best understand the request that the Father *glorify* the Son if we understand it as compassing both the impending death and its glorious sequel in resurrection power and ascension majesty. The crisis is here. Jesus anticipates the Father's approval as He Himself continues obedient unto death.

But the glorification of the Son cannot be conceived independently of the glorification of the Father. The latter is spelled out in terms of the fulfillment of the divine purpose—the securing of *eternal life* for the objects of God's saving mercy. These are beautifully described as those whom the Father has *given* to the Son (vs. 2, cf. vss. 6, 9, 11, 12, 24). They are the fruit of Christ's labor and travail, fruit which shall remain as a perpetual monument to His love and fidelity. Their title to eternal life is the simple faith which has given them a true knowledge of God in Christ. The world by its wisdom does not arrive at this knowledge (I Cor. 1: 21), but the believer finds God in Jesus Christ (vs. 3; cf. 1:18).

The Father gave something else to the Son besides His people, and the very fact that the verb *gave* is used for this work of redemption is significant (vs. 4). Without the finished work there could not be a gathered people. At the moment of utterance the work was not finished, but for Jesus the Cross and its triumph was an ever-present now. What sublime confidence that nothing could keep Him from enduring the Cross! Out of this confidence He prays that the Father will glorify Him, granting Him a return to that original glory shared by Father and Son (cf. 1:1, 2). It was a modest petition, for actually our Lord was to re-enter this glory laden with the tokens of His victory, triumphant over all the hosts of evil, possessing a name above every name. But simply to be restored to the Father's presence—this was the longing desire of the Son away from Home.

Next the thoughts of the Lord turn to His chosen followers who still surround Him, but only as they are connected with His mission (vss. 6-8). This section is therefore transitional. Here Jesus states in simple terms what He has done for these men and what their response has been. He has manifested the Father and communicated to them the words the Father has given. The disciples' response is set forth in four key verbs—*received, believed, known, kept*. This last is most remarkable. How could our Lord assert that these men, so dull of understanding, so prone to selfish ambition, had kept His word? He is a generous judge, reading the underlying sentiment of the heart where loyalty has its root. In comparison with others, this chosen company had indeed kept His word, and Jesus was grateful.

Intercession proper begins with the Lord's declaration that He is praying for His own (vs. 9). His exclusion of the world is not to be understood as indication that He has abandoned the world because it has refused Him. By no means had all the world so much as heard of Him or His claims. Just as the disciples were essential to the Spirit's work of convicting the world (16:7, 8), so they are necessary to Christ's plan

101

of reaching the world with the knowledge of His salvation. Scripture has little in it about praying for the unsaved, but much about praying for those who are to be witnesses to the unsaved.

As the Good Shepherd, Jesus feels His heart going out to those men who from the human standpoint seem so few, so forlorn. He asks that the Father *keep* them (cf. 10:28-29). No longer will this little flock be able to see Him up ahead, calling them to follow (10:4). They are committed now to the tender care of the Father who neither slumbers nor sleeps. The wolf who seeks to ravage the flock is the evil one (vs. 15). With Satan's deadly snares in view, Jesus had already prayed for Peter's deliverance (Luke 22:31-32). The others would have their turn, and they needed divine protection. Since they belong to the Father and have been given to the Son, Jesus can the more readily pray this prayer. But He cannot include Judas, for he does not belong, for he is *the son of perdition* (vs. 12). As the disciples are in the world but not of it, so is Judas in the apostolic company but not of it. There must be honesty in prayer as in all else. Jesus knows the man is *lost,* so He does not include him. We lack knowledge of this sort, so our prayers should have no bounds.

What an encouragement to be sustained by the prayer of the Son of God! One can stay in the world (vs. 15), and endure to be *hated* by the world (vs. 14), when he knows that the Lord is standing by. This is enough to bring His gift of *joy* to fullness (vs. 13).

A second petition rises from the lips of the Saviour

—*sanctify them* (vs. 17). It is flanked on either side by mention of *the world*. The disciples are not of the world, yet they are sent into the world to do their work. Lest they forget their dissimilarity to the world and so lose the sharp edge of their testimony, they need to be sanctified, that is, consecrated or set apart. The instrument in this ministry of regulation and control is *the truth*. Jesus has spoken it, the Holy Spirit will recall it and guide more deeply into its meaning. All this is necessary to make the call to Christ's service ever compelling, ever thrilling. Fidelity to this task is made infinitely easier by the realization of the privilege involved. Jesus affirms a parallel between His sending of the disciples into the world and the Father's sending of Him (vs. 18). Nothing glorifies the mission as much as this epochal fact.

In connection with the third petition, that they may be *one,* Jesus includes in the scope of His prayer those who will be won to Himself by the consecrated testimony of His immediate followers (vss. 20-21). The inclusion of both groups is given prominence by the word *all* (vs. 21). In a few weeks' time the answer began to be realized. The life of the Church after Pentecost is spelled out in such terms as "together," "with one accord," "of one heart and of one soul." The apostles manifest no airs over the fact that they were the original followers, and the newly born show no envy that they were not numbered among the earliest believers.

It might be thought that this unity is something so sacred and sweet as to be an end in itself, but in this context Jesus sees it as a means for impressing the world in behalf of Himself and His mission (vs. 21). Men plead this consideration today as a reason for chiding divided Christendom and hastening it into visible union of its various branches. Can we really be sure that the world will come to greater faith by such a move? Not by the move itself, for in the Middle Ages men clung to the church when it was visibly one less from love of its fellowship than from fear of provoking its displeasure and experiencing its excommunicating power. But a unity of love will accomplish what no organized movement can effect (13:35).

It is undeniable that this desire for unity among the saints lay upon the heart of the Intercessor as a heavy burden, for He mentions it over and over (vss. 11, 21, 22, 23). We can understand why when we hear the Saviour affirm that this is the nature of the relation between Father and Son (vs. 11). Yet the Church is not merely to find in the Godhead the model for its own life, to be achieved by emulation. In the sovereign and gracious purpose of God, the earthly family of God is given a share in the divine life (*one in us,* vs. 21). To achieve this, the Lord Jesus has conveyed to His people the *glory* given to Him (vs. 22), which seems to mean a share in sonship. He is not ashamed to call them His brethren (20:17). He who sanctifies and they who are sanctified are all of one (Heb. 2:11).

A final request looks beyond the others—that these believing men may be permitted to share the lot of the Lord in the great future that now lies concealed, and that they be enabled to behold His *glory*—not that of divine sonship only, but of that accrued glory that will be His as Redeemer, as Victor, as King and Lord of all (vs. 24). Such a request breathes the undying love of Christ for His own. He would have them experience that eternal love of the Father for Himself, not just to see it (vs. 24), but to know it in themselves as the gift of God in Christ (vs. 26).

IV. The Witness of the Son of God in Obedience to the Father unto Death (18:1—19:42)

1. **The Betrayal and Arrest (18:1-14).** Strengthened by the sublime prayer, Jesus and His followers *went forth.* Prayer gives way to action. By moving into the Garden of Gethsemane, Jesus was advancing to meet His great ordeal, for Judas was well acquainted with this spot and could reasonably count on Jesus seeking it out as He so often did after His day's work of teaching in the temple. The garden lay across the Cedron (Kidron A.S.V.) to the east of the city and is resorted to in our time by hosts of Christian pilgrims.

John gives no account of the Saviour's agony, though he has remarked on Jesus' troubled spirit earlier in the evening, linking it with the betrayal (13:21). He has also magnified the place of prayer as a preparation for the bitter experience awaiting our Lord (chap. 17).

The rulers of the Jews, having cunningly paid Judas in advance, so that he would feel honor bound to fulfill his promise to betray the Lord, saw to it that he was also made to feel the importance of his role as the key man in a large company which had orders to act only at the execution of the given signal. The *band* refers to a detachment of Roman soldiers quartered at the castle of Antonia adjacent to the temple area. These were made available when the Jewish authorities asked for them in the interest of public order and safety. They were supplemented on this occasion by *officers* who were in the employ of the temple hierarchy as police in the sacred precincts (cf. 7:32). Many, if not all, were armed.

Jesus was not taken by surprise (vs. 4). He knew why Judas had left the Upper Room. As Elisha had followed in his heart the movements of his faithless servant Gehazi, so had Jesus been aware of these nocturnal measures designed to capture Him. *Knowing* what was coming, He went forth (cf. vs. 1) to meet this motley throng with a question which seemed to disconcert His captors. *Whom seek ye?* It was unexpected. Even more so was the ready admission of His identity. The effect was stunning. Here were officers who had been sent before to take this man and had been strangely frustrated, returning empty-handed. The soldiers had heard of Jesus and of His miraculous powers. Momentarily all were frozen to the spot, then fell back to the ground. The majesty of the Nazarene had unnerved them. Jesus made use of this dismay and hesitation to secure the freedom of the disciples, at the same time fairly thrusting Himself on His captors. He would bear His trial and suffering alone, even as He had prayed alone in the garden.

Peter's intrusion threatened to change this pattern. His sword flashed and off went an ear from the high priest's servant. Peter had been asleep moments before and had not regained steadiness. His aim was poor. The act drew a rebuke. Christ was not seeking defenders or planning flight. Rather, He was preparing to take the first sips from *the cup* of trial ordained for Him by the Father (vs. 11). This reference to the cup is evidence of John's familiarity with the Synoptic tradition of the Gethsemane experience.

Though making no resistance, Jesus was *bound,* the first of many indignities to be visited upon Him in the coming hours. The next was the requirement to appear before Annas, father-in-law of the current high priest. Annas was crafty and cruel. He had looked forward to the day when he could gloat over this Galilean prophet who had dared to challenge the priestly control of the temple by cleansing it of its merchandising.

2. The Master and the Disciple on Trial (18:15-27). It seems that the sacred record weaves these two accounts together in order to emphasize the difference. Jesus speaks the truth while Peter prevaricates. Jesus is solicitous for the disciples (Peter included), so refuses to say anything about them lest He make trouble for them. But Peter has no concern for the Lord. His only anxiety is for his own safety. His failure seems almost incredible, but several things contributed to it— his boast that he would not fail the Lord (Matt. 26: 33), his inability to remain alert in prayer in the garden, his wild sword-play which called attention to him (vs. 26), his insistence on exposing himself by venturing into the courtyard and mingling with the officers around the fire, all this no doubt in order to try to prove his fidelity to his word and to his position of leadership in the apostolic band. Pride goes before a fall. How humiliating it must have been to fall before the half-playful accusation of a serving maid. Once entangled in his own deceitfulness, Peter could not extricate himself. One denial followed another—then the cock crowing (vs. 27).

Another disciple, doubtless John the apostle, because of his acquaintance with the high priest, was able to enter the chamber where Jesus was being interrogated after removal to the house of Caiaphas (vs. 24). It is probable, then, that by mentioning the high priest (vs. 19), John intends Caiaphas. Otherwise he gives no real account of what happened before the official head of the Sanhedrin. Even so, the report is very scanty. The explanation may be found in the earlier chapters where Jesus has deliberately placed Himself on trial before the nation, presenting the evidences bearing on His person and work. The failure of the nation to receive His testimony makes unnecessary any lengthy examination. The issue has already been decided. Jesus' manner shows that He has no hope of receiving a fair hearing (vss. 20-21).

3. **The Trial before Pilate** (18:28—19:16). Jesus was brought before the Roman governor at an *early* hour in order to hasten His fate before any movement in His favor could gather force among the people. To preserve their ceremonial cleanness, the Jewish leaders refused to enter the Gentile hall of judgment. It is now widely accepted, on the basis of archaeological research, that the building was a part of the

Antonia Castle installations. The Pavement (mentioned in 19:13) has been excavated. This ceremonial scruple of the Jews, which exceeded their concern for justice, compelled Pilate to shift position as he talked to them and then to Jesus, who stood inside.

Coupled with the Jews' stiffness on this point was their impertinence toward Pilate, whom they disliked (vss. 29-31). They wanted the governor to accept their word that the prisoner deserved death and give his approval without reviewing the case in detail. This he could not do by reason of his position. Roman justice must be served.

Much as the Jews wished to accomplish Jesus' death, they were impotent, because the Romans held the power of capital punishment in their own hands (vs. 31). This circumstance worked toward the fulfillment of Jesus' predictions on the manner of His death (vs. 32; cf. 12:32, 33; Matt. 20:19). John's account does not detail for the reader the accusations of the Jews, but presupposes a knowledge of the Synoptic material (Luke 23:2) which includes the allegation that Jesus claimed He was a king. Pilate could not ignore this, because of its possible revolutionary implications. So he interrogated Jesus in private on this score (vs. 33).

Jesus felt obliged to question Pilate on one point (vs. 34). He knew the duplicity of the Jewish leaders. Jesus' claim to be Messiah involved kingship, but not in a military or revolutionary sense. He must make it clear to the governor that His kingdom was *not of this world* (cf. 17:14). He had no desire to gain and wield temporal power. Though He had *servants*, He

110

had not trained them to *fight* (vs. 36). His kingship lay in a different realm. He claimed to be Lord of *truth*. This was no despotic claim, for the truth in Jesus was designed to set men free from the tyranny of sin (cf. 8:32-36).

The conversation was rapidly getting beyond Pilate's depth. With a shrug, this man of affairs asked, *What is truth?* and walked away from the presence of the one Person in the world who could have given him a genuinely satisfying answer. At least he had learned enough to be sure that Jesus was not a dangerous aspirant for political domination who was eager to turn the masses against Rome. He found *no fault* in terms of the charge made by the chief priests.

Pilate thought he knew a way to free Jesus and at the same time please the Jewish populace, if not their leaders. It was a yearly custom at Passover time that he release to the people a prisoner. Thinking that Jesus was a hero with the throng, Pilate felt sure they would ask for His release, but he did not reckon sufficiently with the determination of the Jewish rulers, who possessed a hold over the people sufficient to sway them in a matter of this kind. To Pilate's surprise, Barabbas the notorious criminal was preferred over Jesus (vs. 40). *Robber* means more than thief. This man was an inveterate brigand who knew how to kill and destroy (cf. Acts 3:14).

Having failed in one attempt to release Jesus, Pilate tried another. He reasoned that pity might be aroused in the hearts of the people if he had Jesus scourged. The soldiers entered with zest into the plan, making sport with the prisoner. And cruel sport it was, so that when they were finished blood ran from the sharp pricklings of the crown of thorns and bruises began to show from the blows rained on him. *Behold the man!* Surely Isaiah's prophecy was even then finding fulfillment, that His face would be marred to the point of seeming no longer to belong to a man (Isa. 52: 14). By presenting Him as an object of pity, Pilate hoped to underscore his repeated verdict, *I find no fault in him.* The Galilean little resembled a king now. The stratagem failed, for the hearts of the chief priests and their subordinates were steeled against any plea for mercy. A hoarse cry from many throats rose in the morning air, *Crucify, crucify!*

Angered at their stubbornness, Pilate proposed that they take the prisoner and work their will upon Him, knowing they had not the authority to do it (19:6).

At this point the Jews for the first time revealed their real reason for relentless opposition to Jesus. They considered Him a blasphemer, one who made Himself to be God's Son (vs. 7). It was an old complaint (5:18). These men refused to take Jesus' claims seriously. Son of God! The words sent a chill into the superstitious heart of the governor. So this was why the prisoner was so poised and reserved. He must be planning to retaliate. This could turn out to be a dangerous business. Better face it with a bold front, he told himself. So he began to talk of his authority (vs. 10). Quietly the Lord from Heaven reminded him that he did not have the highest place in the universe. If

112

God's will were not being accomplished, the proceedings would not have gone even this far. But the divine purpose does not excuse the human sin which accomplishes its ends. Pilate's sin is one of injustice. The one who handed Jesus over to the governor (is Caiaphas intended, or Judas?) has sinned more deeply, having rejected God's Anointed. To Pilate it became clearer every minute that the One before him, this Man of mystery, was innocent. So he tried the more strenuously to accomplish His release. But just when he was becoming firm, he collapsed completely before the final blow dealt to him by the chief priests. It was a threat to take the matter to Caesar. He would see it their way. He would recognize how dangerous Jesus was to Roman security. Pilate had such a poor record that he did not dare risk a review of it by the emperor. Justice was in the scales with Pilate's future. His own interests outweighed everything. Weakly the governor sat down. It was the signal that a verdict was near. His last announcement fell flat—*Behold your king!* It was tinged with bitterness. These Jews had outwitted him again. If any satisfaction was to be had in the situation, it came from hearing these rebellious Jews, even though with tongue in cheek, confess that they had no king but Caesar (vs. 15). In rejecting their rightful King, they sold themselves to a pagan monarch. The doom of Israel was sealed in that moment. For all concerned the die was cast. Jesus was ordered to the accursed place of crucifixion and Pilate retired to count the cost of his moral weakness.

4. The Crucifixion (19:17-37).

Part of the ignominy of this form of punishment was the compulsion to bear one's own cross (vs. 17). Luke tells us that another was pressed into service when Jesus' strength failed (Luke 23:26). John gives no details about the two criminals crucified with Jesus (vs. 18). His concern is solely with the central figure. The title placed by Pilate over the cross was not merely an identification; it served to name the accusation against the one condemned. This was a notable prisoner. Because Golgotha was near the city and probably just off the roadway, the inscription was widely read. It created offense among the Jewish leaders, for it seemed to affirm what they denied, that Jesus was actually the national Messiah. But Pilate, so vacillating during the trial, stood firm now. He refused to change the wording (vs. 22).

The events of the hours on the cross are told with brevity and simplicity. First, after the crucifixion itself, comes the parting of the garments, the only things ever taken from Jesus. What He had to give during His life He had given freely—time, counsel, truth, restoration, forgiveness. The distribution of the garments has special importance because it shows again the fulfillment of the prophetic word (Ps. 22:18). God, who knows the end from the beginning, can forecast details hundreds of years beforehand. Naturally the soldiers had no idea they were fulfilling prophecy, yet it had to be (note the *therefore*).

Four women stood near the cross, three of them having the name Mary (vs. 25). With one of them Jesus now concerned Himself, and this concern demonstrates that we cannot read indifference into any of Jesus' relationships with His mother during the course of the ministry. Jesus' love for Mary and His love for John (cf. 13:23) dictated that He should commit each of them to the other. The text suggests that John had a home in Jerusalem (vs. 27; cf. 18:15).

Only once in John's account of the crucifixion is any attention paid to Jesus' suffering, and here again, as His *thirst* is noted, it is for the intent that the fulfillment of Scripture may be observed (Ps. 22:15). Jesus came to honor the Father, and God is honored as His Word is vindicated.

From the wording of the text it seems that Jesus desired a drink chiefly that He might be able to speak out the word of triumph—*it is finished*—the glorious consummation of His mission. All that remained was the delivering up of His spirit to the Father (vs. 30; cf. 10:18). His death was a decision, not a default.

The Jews were anxious that nothing should defile the Passover festivities, and so requested Pilate that the bodies be removed. "This particular night was the beginning both of the Sabbath and of the first and great day of the Passover Festival" (Hoskyns). Once more the circumstances proved to be significant, since Jesus' early death made the breaking of His legs unnecessary. Thus were the Scriptures fulfilled (Ps. 34: 20).

Another detail is noticed, namely, the piercing of the side. John is not interested in the physiology of the spectacle of blood and water but in their theological import. Water signifies cleansing and blood the very life of the Son of God, of which believers partake (6:54, 56). Life and spiritual health are now available, for the Life-giver has poured Himself out for others. This momentous fact must be related to Scripture also, and so it is (Zechariah 12:10).

5. **The Burial** (19:38-42). If discipleship is measured by boldness of identification with Jesus and by personal sacrifice for Him, then Joseph of Arimathaea and Nicodemus must be counted among that noble company. And if love is to be measured by deed rather than by word, then the devotion of these two men was genuine and rare. Joseph's garden and Nicodemus' spices saved the precious form of the Son of man from neglect and desecration. In the silence of the tomb the hours pass. This is the aftermath of the Cross and the womb of the new creation, soon to yield up Him who is the first-begotten from the dead.

V. The Witness of the Risen Lord
(20:1-31)

As a fact of history, the resurrection of Christ was a witness of the Father on behalf of the Son, but the Gospel records, as distinct from the Acts and the Epistles, do not emphasize this. Rather, they narrate the appearances of Jesus to His own and relate how He was able to confirm His claims in their own experience.

1. **The Appearance to Mary Magdalene (20:1-18).** This woman was the first person to see our Lord in His risen state. The privilege was not given to an apostle. What a testimony to Christ's desire to magnify the spirit of democracy in the church! Mary started for the tomb with other women (Mark 16:1). On the way they discussed the problem of the stone which blocked the entrance (Mark 16:3). It was a heavy circular stone which took considerable strength to roll aside. Surprised by the spectacle of the stone already removed, the women concluded that the body of Jesus had been stolen (see the words *we know not* in vs. 2), but Mary alone ran to report the incident to Peter and John, who had been together since the trial of Jesus (cf. 18: 16).

Mary's dismay communicated itself to these disciples, who started for the garden on the run, leaving Mary to follow as well as she could. The beloved disciple arrived first, peered into the tomb and saw the graveclothes, but gained only a general impression of the scene. However, when Peter pushed past him and went inside, John followed and gained a clearer view. The position of the linen cloths, not in disarray, but in order, and especially the location of the headpiece, perched on the slab in a neat, spiral shape, convinced John that there had been no pilfering of the tomb. He *believed* (that Jesus had risen). It was no easy conclusion, for the disciples had not so far understood the teaching of Scripture that Jesus *must rise from the dead.* Jesus had taught them to expect it, but their minds were closed to the possibility of it (Matt. 16:21; Mark 9: 10).

Peter and John left, but Mary could not tear herself away until this mystery of the opened tomb and the missing body was solved. Her tears testify that she still thought of the body as removed by human hands. If only she could see that sacred form again! Still weeping, she stooped and peered into the sepulcher much as John had done. But she saw a sight not granted to him—angels stationed where Jesus' head and feet had been (vs. 12). To Mary they provided neither fear nor glamor. Her mind was preoccupied with thoughts of what had befallen the body of Jesus.

Still weeping, she turned away back into the garden. That must be the gardener, she thought, as a form presented itself in the early morning light. Perhaps he knew something. It may be that she had been wrong in thinking enemies had stolen the body. No harm would be done in questioning him (vs. 15). A greater than the gardener is here! Mary! No one could speak her name that way but Jesus. Tears of sorrow became instantly tears of joy. Master! Yes, to all His other masteries He had added the mastery of death.

Mary's cry of glad recognition was accompanied by a quick movement. Evidently she laid hold of Jesus as though to retain Him and keep Him ever near. The words *touch me not* really mean, Stop holding me. Jesus belongs to Heaven now, even though He consents to tarry here for a few days. Mary must go with the tidings of resurrection and impending ascension to Jesus' brethren—not James and the other kin of Jesus, but the disciples (cf. Matthew 12:49). The first command of the risen Lord is *go and say,* and so is the last before the ascension (Acts 1:8). Mary is the first witness of the resurrection, and the first emissary of the risen Saviour.

2. The Appearance to the Ten Disciples (20:19-23). Death had not fundamentally changed Jesus' relation to these men. He came to them without announcement and without invitation. Inevitably He took His rightful place at once *in the midst* (cf. Luke 2:46; John 19:18). His word of *peace* was two-edged, allaying their fear of the Jews and their sense of shame at having deserted Him in the garden. Already the disciples were able to draw upon the legacy lately promised to them (14:27).

The showing of His hands and side confirmed the identity which His manner and His words had already certified. Moreover, this act was an invitation to share with Him the joy of His triumph over death (vs. 20).

Almost immediately, however, the Master recalls the minds of His followers to His mission and their part in it. What we have here is a kind of postscript to the Upper Room Discourse and the Prayer, with great prominence given to the sending forth of the apostles on the model of Jesus' commission from the Father (vs. 21; cf. 17:18).

This is a crucial point in redemption history, the beginning of the new creation. *He breathed on them* (vs. 22; cf. Gen. 2:7). Answering to the breath of life in the old creation is the Holy Spirit in the new. The sin which spoiled the old creation has now found a remedy. These men are to apply it by their preaching of the Gospel. If men refuse the remedy, their sins are *retained;* if they receive the Lord, their sins are *remitted* (forgiven). But no mission is attempted until the Lord ascends and the Spirit comes upon the apostles in power (cf. 7:37-39).

3. The Appearance to the Eleven Disciples (20: 24-29). Thomas is prominent here, due to his absence on the former occasion. It should be recognized that he did not flatly refuse to accept the resurrection. What he demanded was incontestable evidence, personally experienced (his finger, the Lord's wounds). The circumstances were identical with those of the previous appearance—the shut doors, the suddenly appearing Saviour and the greeting of *peace* (vs. 26).

Jesus uses language designed to show that He is

fully aware of Thomas' words (vs. 27). This can well serve as a reminder that Christ, though unseen, knows what we speak, even when it is voiced to others rather than to Himself. His invitation to Thomas was apparently not accepted. Thomas did not need to touch the Lord. To see was sufficient (vs. 29). With a cry of recognition and acknowledgment, he voiced his faith in the highest possible terms (vs. 28). In receiving the testimony, Jesus nevertheless pointed out the blessedness of those who lack physical contact, such as Thomas had enjoyed, and yet believe (vs. 29; cf. I Peter 1:8). To act as Thomas did after the Lord was withdrawn from the world would make faith impossible. Men should be willing to believe—on the basis of adequate testimony (cf. Mark 16:14).

4. The Purpose of This Book (20:30-31).

Since the previous incident involved the greatest sign of all, the resurrection, and magnified the necessity for faith, and contained a towering testimony to the person of Christ, the way was prepared for this summary statement. More signs were wrought, but no more are needed for faith. This has been amply demonstrated by the multitudes who have come to the place of faith through reading the Gospel according to John. The signs are not to be valued in themselves, but as pointers directing the reader to Christ. He is the object of faith. God honors that faith by granting life, something no sign in itself can give.

VI. Epilogue (21:1-25)

This last section of the book is concerned with a further disclosure of the risen Lord to certain disciples, followed by a closing word about the writer. The incident has three phases: a fishing expedition, a dialogue between Jesus and Simon Peter, and finally a prophecy of Peter's future. Peter's prominence is apparent throughout, overshadowed only by that of the Lord Himself.

These resurrection appearances were occasions when Jesus showed *Himself*. In Luke's account teaching is strongly featured, but here, agreeably to the Christocentric purpose of the Fourth Gospel, the person of Christ is central.

The setting is the sea of Tiberias, another name for the sea of Galilee, derived from Tiberias, a large town on the western shore. Simon Peter was finding inactivity hard to bear, especially when the visits from the Lord were many days apart. The sight of the water and his boat moored not far away was too much for him! *I go a fishing.* Evidently there was no thought of a return to this occupation on a permanent basis, otherwise the rest would not have agreed to go with him. That he should desert his calling after seeing the Lord and being forgiven for his denial (Luke 24:34) is unthinkable.

Doubtless we are intended to detect a spiritual truth behind this story. *They caught nothing* despite their tackle and experience and a propitious time—the night. All was changed when the weary fishermen hearkened to the directions of the stranger who stood on the shore a hundred yards or so from the boat. At once their fortune changed and the boat became the scene of feverish activity. The beloved disciple perceived that the stranger was the Lord. His presence, coupled with obedience to His command, had meant the exchange of failure for success. He had warned earlier that apart from Him His followers could do nothing (15:5). Here was a demonstration of it.

By an easy and natural transition we come to the following episode—the breakfast at the lakeside and the conversation between Jesus and Peter. The disciple's haste to get ashore and meet with the Lord (vs. 7) hints at his eagerness to see the Master. It may be that the miracle recalled to his mind a similar experience in this area which led to his enlistment as a disciple (Luke 5:1-11).

The same Lord who prospers His own in their work is able to meet their personal needs. Here was a fire of coals, with fish being broiled over it, and a supply of bread. Jesus' invitation to bring the fish (which He graciously insists they had caught) seems designed to make the disciples feel that what they had was to be pooled with the Lord's provision. Actually the fish were not needed at the moment and could be sold to meet the temporal wants of the men.

Not yet had the disciples become fully accustomed

to being in the presence of the risen Master. A sense of strain seemed upon them as they ate in silence (vs. 12). Jesus seemed to hold Himself somewhat at a distance (cf. 20:17 and the words in Luke 24:44, "while I was yet with you," as though that era had closed). As in dealing with Mary Magdalene, so it is with this circle of seven. No time is spent on pleasantries.

The closing of the meal was the signal for the opening of an unusual conversation between the Lord and Peter. It was an inquisition rather than a conversation. Jesus seems hard on the disciple who had failed. Yet His purpose was just as full of love as His question. As a believer, Peter had already been forgiven his sin of a few weeks before, but as the Lord's servant he needs restoration in the presence of his brethren, the very men he had wronged by asserting a greater devotion to Jesus than they could muster (Matt. 26:31-33). This is the point of the question, *Lovest thou me more than these?* (vs. 15). We may feel justified in comparing our gifts or our achievements with those of others, though this is dangerous. But to compare our loyalty and by inference our love is positively wrong. There is a latent rebuke in the Saviour's question.

When the question had been propounded the third time, Peter had had enough. Magnificent in the midst of his admonition, he appeals at last from his own awareness that he loves the Lord to the Lord's own perfect knowledge—*thou knowest that I love thee.* Only a man with a good conscience, a man who knows the heart of the Son of God, dares to speak in this fashion.

Each time Peter affirms his love for Christ he is given a sphere of service—to feed Christ's lambs, to tend His sheep, to feed the sheep. But we must not overlook the possessive pronoun—*my* lambs, *my* sheep. In love Christ laid down His life for these. He will not entrust the care of them to anyone who does not love Him. The under-shepherd must have a heart for Christ. If he does, he will have a heart also for the sheep who are so precious to the Son of God.

Christ assumes that Peter is accepting the commission, though the disciple says nothing. In faithfulness the Lord would have His servant count the cost of discipleship. Ahead looms death, and from the description of it Peter learns that he will die as the Saviour died, by crucifixion (vss. 18-19). Christ glorified the Father by His death. Peter will do the same. Death becomes a triumph. And it is not coming at once, but only when Peter is *old*. A vista of service is granted here before the final sacrifice.

Recalling Peter from dreams of the future to the needs of the present, Jesus launched him on a new era of work with the same summons which opened the first phase three years before—*follow me* (vs. 19).

Then Peter did a very human thing. Taking his eyes off Jesus, he looked toward John, his familiar friend. A question rose spontaneously to his lips. He was bound to find out, if he could, what was the Saviour's plan for John (vs. 21). But it was a diversion from his own orders and an intrusion into the privacy of John's place in the plans of Jesus. Jesus' answer reveals that His will for one life may be quite different

125

from His will for another. John did not live till the coming of Christ (Jesus did not say he would), but he did tarry to a good old age. Tradition tells us that he died a natural death after a long and useful life.

Verse 24 seems to be an endorsement of the writer by those who know him personally. They respect his desire to remain anonymous but they emphasize his qualification. His *testimony* is *true*. He writes as a personal witness of the things described in this book.

Finally, John resumes the pen to tell us that the deeds of Jesus recorded in this book are but a fraction of the whole. But if they all could be recorded, they would not change the story, but would merely add extra weight to the testimony. Jesus has been sufficiently set forth. The writer can stay his pen. He has done well. Every believing soul gladly echoes his *Amen*.

BIBLIOGRAPHY

Barclay, William. *The Gospel of John* (The Daily Study Bible). Philadelphia: Westminster Press, 2nd edition, 2 vols., 1956.

Barrett, C. K. *The Gospel According to St. John.* London: S.P.C.K., 1955.

Bernard, T. D. *The Central Teaching of Jesus Christ.* New York: Macmillan and Co., 1892.

Dodd, C. H. *The Interpretation of the Fourth Gospel.* Cambridge: The University Press, 1953.

Dods, Marcus. *The Gospel of St. John* (*The Expositor's Bible*). New York: A. C. Armstrong and Son, 2 vols., 1902. Reprinted by Wm. B. Eerdmans Publishing Co.

Godet, F. *Commentary on the Gospel of John.* Edinburgh: T. and T. Clark, 3rd edition, 3 vols., 1895. Reprinted by Zondervan Publishing House.

Hendriksen, William. *Exposition of the Gospel According to John.* Grand Rapids: Baker Book House, 2 vols., 1953.

Hoskyns, E. C. *The Fourth Gospel.* London: Faber and Faber, Ltd., 2nd edition, 1947. Reprinted by Allenson.

Howard, W. F. *Christianity According to St. John.* London: Duckworth, 1943.

Lenski, R. C. H. *The Interpretation of St. John's Gospel.* Columbus: Lutheran Book Concern, 1942.

Milligan, William and Moulton, William F. *Commentary on the Gospel of St. John.* Edinburgh: T. and T. Clark, 1898.

Reith, George. *The Gospel According to St. John.* Edinburgh: T. and T. Clark, 2 vols., 1889.

Tenney, Merrill C., *John: The Gospel of Belief*. Grand Rapids: Wm. B. Eerdmans Publishing Co., 1948.

Westcott, B. F. *The Gospel According to St. John*. London: John Murray, 1882. Reprinted by Wm. B. Eerdmans Publishing Co.

Moody Press, a ministry of the Moody Bible Institute, is designed for education, evangelization and edification. If we may assist you in knowing more about Christ and the Christian life, please write us without obligation to: Moody Press, c/o MLM, Chicago, Illinois 60610.